PATCHWORK
for Your Home

ONDORI

CONTENTS

★ Copyright © 1984 Ondorisha Publishers Ltd., All Rights Reserved.
★ Published by Ondorisha Publishers Ltd.,
   32 Nishigoken-cho, Shinjuku-ku, Tokyo 162, Japan.
★ Sole Overseas Distributor: Japan Publications Trading Co., Ltd.
   P.O. Box 5030 Tokyo International, Tokyo, Japan.
★ Distributed in the United States by Kodansha International/USA Ltd. through Harper & Row,
   Publishers, Inc., 10 East 53rd Street, New York, New York 10022.
   Australia by Bookwise International, 1 Jeanes Street, Beverley, South Australia 5009,
   Australia.

10 9 8 7 6 5 4 3 2

ISBN 0-87040-585-3
Printed in Japan

CLASSIC PATCHWORK

EIGHT-POINTED STAR TABLECLOTH

Instructions on page 2.

Fabrics Used (Actual Size)

ⓐ   ⓑ   ⓒ   ⓓ   ⓔ   ⓕ

MATERIALS

FABRICS: (a) 90 cm by 135 cm; (b) 90 cm by 70 cm; (c)-(f) 40 cm by 25 cm each; cotton fabric for lining, 123 cm by 98 cm. Thin quilt batting, 98 cm by 123 cm. White and dark brown quilting thread.

FINISHED SIZE: 123 cm by 98 cm.

DIRECTIONS:

1. Cut out patches and sew them together by hand. Make 6 blocks. Then assemble blocks with borders.

2. Transfer quilting patterns to borders. Draw diamond patterns, moving template as indicated.
3. Pin and baste top, batting and lining together. Quilt along quilting lines, starting from center toward each side.
4. Bind edges to finish.

Cutting

Top   See next page for eight-pointed star patterns.
Add 0.7 cm seam allowance all around unless otherwise indicated.

Quilt batting   123 cm × 98 cm

Lining (cotton fabric)   123 cm × 98 cm

No seam allowance along edges to be bound.

Corner

Wrong side
Slip-stitch
Fold
1.5 cm

Strip for binding

5
b
$\frac{125}{98}$ } Cut 2 each

Patterns for Eight-pointed Star Block (Actual size)   Add 0.7cm seam allowance.

[Quilt with white quilting thread]

a Cut 24 pieces

a Cut 24 pieces

c ~ f
Cut 12 pieces each

Quilting patterns
(Actual size)

Quilt with
dark brown thread.

Center

Quilt with
white quilting thread.

Quilting Pattern for Side.

3

Fabrics Used (Actual Size)

ⓐ
ⓑ
ⓒ
ⓓ
ⓔ
ⓕ
ⓖ
ⓗ
ⓘ

5

MATERIALS

FABRICS: (a)-(f) silk crepe, 50 cm by 15 cm; (g) silk crepe, 15 cm square; (h) for lining, 1 m by 2 m; (i) for binding, 90 cm by 20 cm. Quilt batting, 1 m square. White and black quilting thread.

FINISHED SIZE: 1 m square.

DIRECTIONS:

1. Cut out patches for fans. Sew 6 patches together by hand.
2. Appliqué pieced fans in place with slip stitch.
3. Transfer quilting patterns.
4. Pin and baste top, batting and lining together. Quilt along quilting lines, starting from center outward. Embroider ribs of fans in chain stitch.
5. Bind edges to finish.

Cut 1 each from (h) for top and lining.

24

Quilt with black quilting thread.

Circle with 28 cm radius.

Quilt with white quilting thread.

Circle with 626.5 cm radius.

a b c d e f

g

25 25

100

Appliqué in slip-stitch

a b c d e f

47.5

100

Binding

See page 18 for mitered corner.

Binding strip

4

i

405

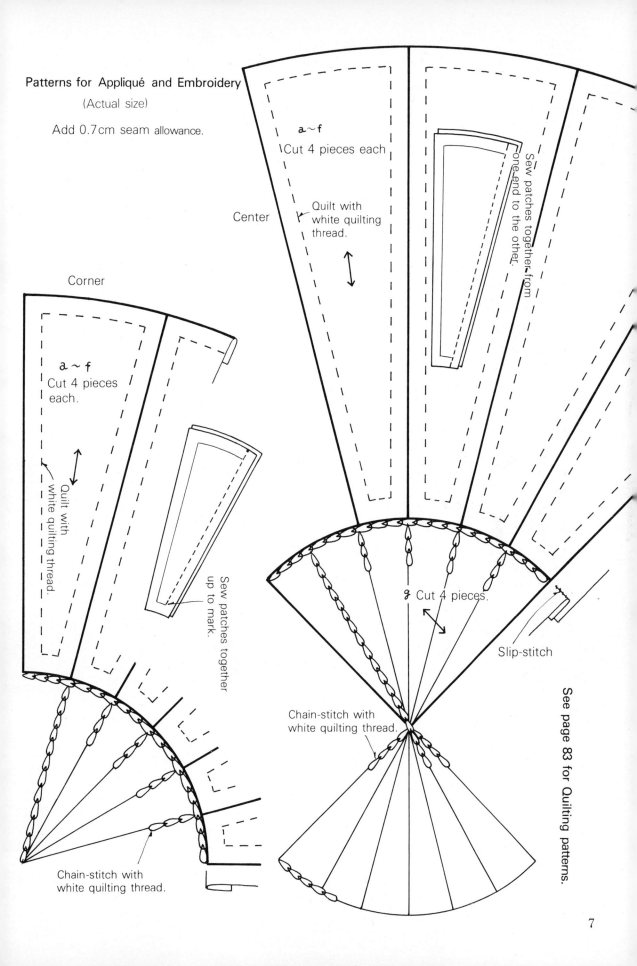

Patterns for Appliqué and Embroidery

(Actual size)

Add 0.7cm seam allowance.

Center

a ~ f
Cut 4 pieces each

Quilt with
white quilting
thread.

Corner

a ~ f
Cut 4 pieces
each.

Quilt with
white quilting thread.

Sew patches together
up to mark.

Sew patches together from
one end to the other.

g Cut 4 pieces.

Slip-stitch

Chain-stitch with
white quilting thread.

Chain-stitch with
white quilting thread.

See page 83 for Quilting patterns.

7

Fabrics Used (Actual Size)

| a | b | c | d | e | f | g |

PILLOWS

Instructions on page 10.

MATERIALS

FABRICS FOR LEFT PILLOW: (a) 75 cm by 46 cm; (b) 33 cm square; (c, d, e, f) 17 cm square each; (g) 24 cm by 16 cm; for lining (a) 45 cm square.

FABRICS FOR RIGHT PILLOW: (2) 80 cm by 46 cm; (1) 90 cm by 20 cm; (3-38) small amount each of 36 different prints; for lining (1) 45 cm square. Quilt batting, 45 cm square. Quilting thread: white for left pillow and white & black for right pillow. 35 cm zipper. 45 cm-square inner pillow stuffed with kapok.

FINISHED SIZE: 43.5 cm square.

DIRECTIONS:

1. Cut out patches and sew them together by hand.
2. Pin and baste top, batting and lining together. Quilt.
3. Sew zipper onto back piece with 2 cm seams.
4. With right sides facing, sew front and back pieces together and zigzag-stitch along raw edges by machine. Turn inside out.
5. Insert inner pillow.

Left pillow

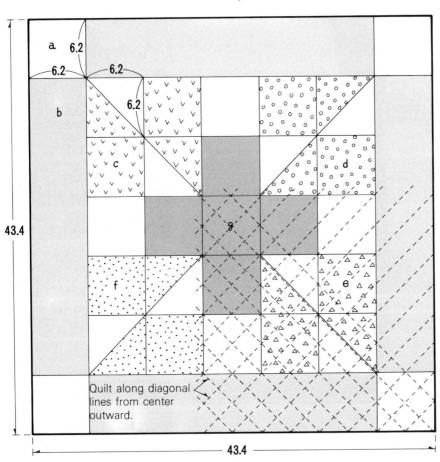

Quilt along diagonal lines from center outward.

Cutting

Top
Front Add 0.7 cm seam
allowance.

	6.2 cm square	6.2 cm triangle
a	8 pieces	8 pieces
c	2 "	2 "
d	2 "	2 "
e	2 "	2 "
f	2 "	2 "
g	5 pieces	
b	6.2 cm × 31 cm 4 pieces	

Cut batting and lining 45 cm square each.

Cut 2 pieces from (a) for back, 46 cm by 25 cm each.

Piecing

Right pillow

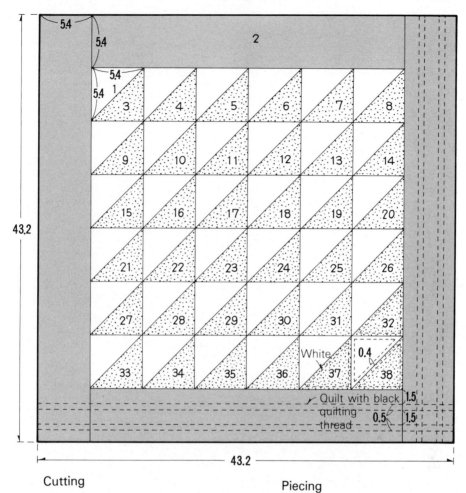

Cutting

Front

Top Add 0.7cm seam allowance.

2	5.4cm × 32.4cm	2 pieces
	5.4cm × 43.2cm	2 pieces
1	5.4cm triangle	36 pieces
3 ~ 38	″	1 piece each

Cut batting and lining 45cm square each.

Cut 2 pieces from (2) for back,
45cm by 25cm each.

Piecing

GRANDMA'S FLOWER GARDEN TABLECLOTH

Instructions on page 14.

Fabrics Used (Actual Size)

ⓐ

ⓓ

ⓑ

ⓒ

Grandma's Flower Garden Tablecloth, shown on pages 12 & 13.

MATERIALS

FABRICS: (a) at least 90 cm by 130 cm (required amount of fabric differs depending on designs); (b) 90 cm by 270 cm; (c) 90 cm by 170 cm; (d) for underlay, 90 cm by 6 m; for lining, 90 cm by 360 cm.

FINISHED SIZE: 176 cm in diameter. (Diameter of underlay is 226 cm.)

DIRECTIONS:

1. Cut out patches and sew them together as shown in diagram. After piecing all patches, cut off excess beyond circle rim.
2. Join pieces for lining. Cut out lining same size as top. With wrong sides together, apply glue between layers in several places.
3. Bind edges with bias-cut strips, showing 1.5 cm binding on front.
4. Cut out fabric for underlay and sew 3 pieces together. Bind edges to finish.

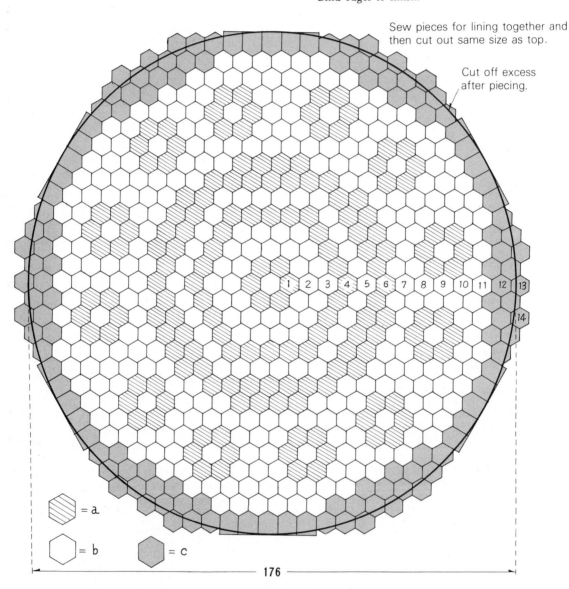

Sew pieces for lining together and then cut out same size as top.

Cut off excess after piecing.

= a
= b   = c

176

Bias-cut strip   Cut 1 piece each.

5

c = **555**   Tablecloth
d = **710**   Underlay

14

Patterns (Actual size)

Add 0.7 cm seam allowance.

a   162 pieces

b   325 pieces

c   96 pieces

c   30 pieces

Piecing (Sew with machine)

Sew patches together in rounds starting from center.
(Sew 6 patches on 1st round and 12 patches on 2nd,
ending with 78 patches on 13th round.
Make 6 groups of 11 patches for last round.)

Machine-stitch piecced patches together
in numerical order from center.

Edge

Turn back seam
allowances and
press.

Press seams
to one side.

Center

Sew between marks on 1st round.
(Don't sew from edge to edge.)
From 2nd round, sew from mark to
edge toward center.

Center
patch   1   2   3

Cutting layout for
underlay

Bias-cut strip

Underlay

d

226
Sew with
1 cm seam
allowance.

1
Seam allowance

70   88   70

Finishing

1. With right sides together,
   sew bias strip
   along edge.   0.1 cm

   Turn back
   1 cm.

2. Turn to right side
   and press.

3.5
cm

3. Machine-stitch

ⓓ   ⓒ   ⓑ   ⓐ

Blue Pillow

YO-YO FLOWER PILLOWS

Instructions on page 18.

ⓔ

ⓕ

ⓖ

ⓗ

ⓘ

ⓙ   ⓚ   ⓛ   ⓜ

16

Orange Pillow

ⓐ ⓑ ⓒ ⓓ ⓔ ⓕ ⓖ ⓗ ⓘ ⓙ ⓚ ⓛ ⓜ

Yo-yo Flower Pillows,

shown on pages 16 & 17.

MATERIALS

FABRICS: (a) 90cm by 42cm; (f, h, i) 22cm by 16cm each; (b, c, d, e, g, j, k, l, m) 20cm square each; for lining, 42cm square. Quilt batting, 42cm square. Six-strand embroidery floss, No. 25; 1/2 skein each of dark and light olive green. White quilting thread. 33cm zipper. Polyester fiberfill. 42cm-square inner pillow stuffed with kapok.

FINISHED SIZE: 42cm square.

DIRECTIONS:

1. Cut out patches for planter and two buds. Sew patches together using cardboard and whip stitch (see page 125). Make flowers following diagrams.

2. Enlarge quilting patterns and transfer to front piece. Mark places for appliques.
3. Appliqué planter with slip stitch and work running stitches along seams of each hexagon.
4. Pin and baste front, batting and lining together. Quilt.
5. Embroider stems. Sew on flowers. Appliqué buds padded with polyester fiberfill using slip stitch.
6. Sew zipper onto back pieces. With wrong sides facing, bind edges of front and back pieces together.

Flower (yo-yo)

Cut out 11cm circle
(including seam allowance).
f h i Cut 2 each
g j k l m Cut 1 each

Making yo-yo flower

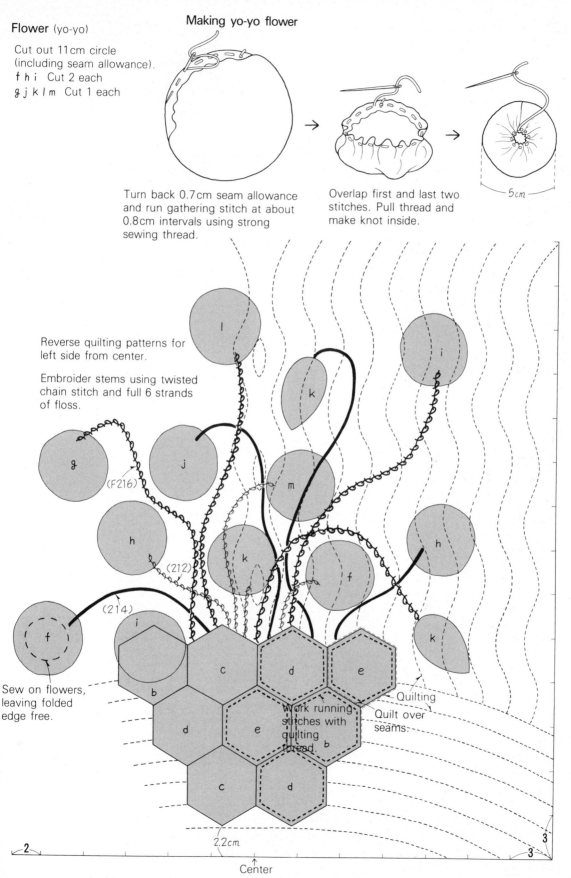

Turn back 0.7cm seam allowance
and run gathering stitch at about
0.8cm intervals using strong
sewing thread.

Overlap first and last two
stitches. Pull thread and
make knot inside.

5cm

Reverse quilting patterns for
left side from center.

Embroider stems using twisted
chain stitch and full 6 strands
of floss.

(F216)

(212)

(214)

Sew on flowers,
leaving folded
edge free.

Quilting

Quilt over
seams

Work running
stitches with
quilting
thread

2.2cm

Center

2

3
3

PINK BOW CRIB QUILT
Instructions on page 22.

Fabrics Used (Actual Size)

ⓐ

ⓑ

ⓒ

ⓓ

ⓔ

Pink Bow Crib Quilt,
shown on pages 20 & 21.

MATERIALS

FABRICS: (a) 90 cm square; (b, c) 90 cm by 45 cm each; (d) 60 cm by 30 cm; (e) 62 cm square; for lining and backing, 104 cm square each. Quilt batting, 104 cm square. DMC Six-strand embroidery floss, No. 25: 1-1/2 skeins each of pink (963), peacock-green (993) and blue (3325); 1 skein each of peacock-green (992) and olive-green (988); 1/2 skein each of peony-rose (602), rose pink (309), pink (225), blue (312), purple (552), brown (975) and white; small amount each of rose-pink (335), peacock-blue (806, 824), purple (209) and dark brown (898).

FINISHED SIZE: 104 cm square.

DIRECTIONS:

1. Cut out patches and appliques. Appliqué as indicated using slip stitch.
2. Transfer enlarged quilting patterns onto fabric (e).
3. Sew patches together by machine.
4. Pin and baste top, batting and backing together. Quilt center design, patches and outlines of appliques.
5. Place quilted piece on lining and bind edges to finish.

Quilting patterns Quilt with 4 strands of floss and back-stitch unless otherwise indicated.

Appliqué

4
3.5
(312)
(602)
20
c
b
20
20
2
Binding

Quilt with running stitch 0.5cm in from seams (993) with 3 strands of floss.

e

Quilt with back stitch.

104

104

Cutting

Top piece (Patchwork)
Add 0.7cm seam allowance.
Cut 8 pieces of 20cm square from (b) and (c).
Cut 60cm square from (e).
Cut batting, backing and lining 104cm square each.

Strip for binding

6

a

418

See page 18 for mitered corner.

Appliqué patterns (Actual size)

Add 0.5cm seam allowance.

a Cut 8

(602) Outline-stitch with 3 strands of floss.

Fold

Quilt close to appliqué using running stitch and 3 strands of floss. (963)

d Cut 8

(312) Outline-stitch with 3 strands of floss.

(3325) 3 strands of floss

Fold

ⓔ　　　　　　ⓕ　　　　　　ⓖ　　　　　　ⓗ

24

*Fabrics Used
(Actual Size)*

ⓐ

ⓑ

ⓒ

ⓓ

ⓘ

ⓙ

ⓚ

ⓛ

25

TABLECLOTH
MATERIALS

FABRICS: (a) 91 cm by 362 cm; (e, f) 84 cm square each; (b, c, d, g, h) 84 cm by 63 cm each. Quilt batting, 120 cm by 350 cm. Olive green sewing thread, No. 30. White and vermilion felt, 20 cm square each. Olive green ribbon, 0.5 cm wide and 5.2 m long. Polyester fiberfill.

FINISHED SIZE: 175 cm square.

DIRECTIONS:

1. Cut out patches and sew them together by machine.
2. Join pieces of batting (see page 125). Join pieces of lining.
3. Pin and baste top, batting and lining together. Quilt by machine.
4. Turn lining over top, turn in seam allowances and machine-stitch.
5. Make radishes and carrots with felt and sew in place.

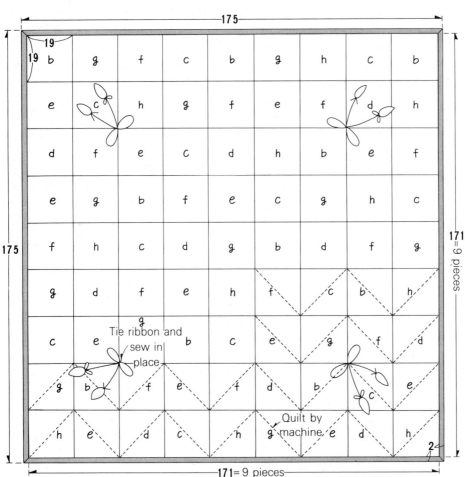

Cutting

Top Cut patches 21 cm square.

bd = 10 pieces each
h = 11 pieces
cg = 12 pieces each
ef = 13 pieces each

Batting Sew 2 pieces of 120 cm by 175 cm together and cut into 175 cm square.

Lining Cut out 2 pieces of 91 cm by 181 cm from (a) and sew them together with 0.5 cm seams to make 181 cm square.

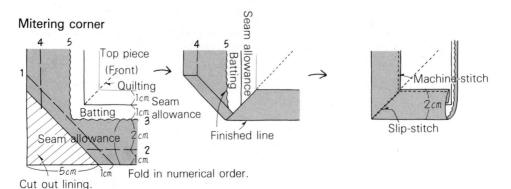

Mitering corner

Top piece (Front)
Quilting
1 cm Seam allowance
1 cm allowance
Batting
Seam allowance
2 cm
5 cm   1 cm   Fold in numerical order.
Cut out lining.

Seam allowance
Batting
Finished line

Machine-stitch
2 cm
Slip-stitch

Patterns for Carrot and Radish

(Actual size)

Felt

White
Vermilion } Cut 8 each

How to make carrot and radish

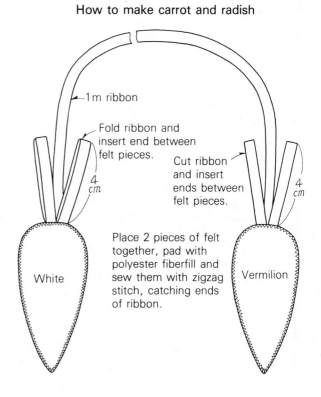

1m ribbon

Fold ribbon and
insert end between
felt pieces.

Cut ribbon
and insert
ends between
felt pieces.

4 cm

4 cm

White

Vermilion

Place 2 pieces of felt
together, pad with
polyester fiberfill and
sew them with zigzag
stitch, catching ends
of ribbon.

PILLOW
MATERIALS
FABRICS FOR RADISH: (a) 73 cm by 48 cm; (b, c, d, e, g) 27 cm by 14 cm each; (f, h) 14 cm square each; (i) 11 cm by 5 cm; (j) 10 cm square.
FOR CARROT: (a) 73 cm by 48 cm; (c, e, f, g, h) 27 cm by 14 cm each; (b, d) 14 cm square each; (k) 9 cm by 5 cm; (l) 17 cm square. Six-strand embroidery floss, No. 25: white and dark green for radish; red and green for carrot. 30 cm zipper. 48 cm-square inner pillow stuffed with kapok. Polyester fiberfill.
FINISHED SIZE: 46 cm square.
DIRECTIONS:
1. Cut out patches and sew them together by machine.
2. Appliqué and embroider in place.
3. Sew on zipper. With right sides facing, sew front and back pieces together. Turn inside out.
4. Insert inner pillow.

Cutting
Front (patchwork)   Add 1 cm seam allowance.
  Back   Cut 48 cm square from (a).

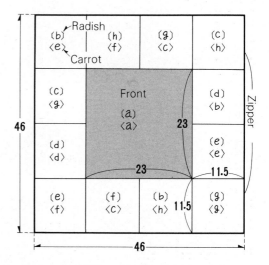

See page 84 for Appliqué patterns.

Patchwork *Gifts*

HOUSE WALL HANGING

Instructions on page 85.

Instructions on page 85.

STUFFED ANIMALS (RABBITS AND HORSES)

Instructions on page 30.

Instructions on page 30.

MATERIALS
FOR BIG HORSE
FABRIC: Cotton fabric: (a) 50cm by 30cm; (b-g) Small amount of each. Polyester fiberfill. Six-strand embroidery floss, No. 25: Beige and yellow. Beige looped yarn. Scrap of light brown felt. 2 black beads.

FOR SMALL HORSE
FABRIC: Unbleached sheeting, 45cm by 20cm; cotton broadcloth, small amount each of red and red with white dots. Red embroidery floss, No. 25. 1 skein of basting thread. Scrap of red felt. Polyester fiberfill. 8 gold beads, 0.6cm in diameter; 2 black beads.

FOR RABBIT
FABRIC: Cotton fabric: FOR GREEN RABBIT: (a) 40cm square; (b-e) small amount each. FOR BLUE RABBIT: Blue, 20cm by 15cm; small amount each of 11 different prints. FOR RED RABBIT: Red, 32cm by 18cm; small amount each of red with white dots and red with floral design. 3 black beads for each. Black sewing thread. Six-strand embroidery floss, No. 25: Small amount each of red and white. Red pencil.

FINISHED SIZE: See diagram for HORSE. GREEN RABBIT, 28cm tall. BLUE AND RED RABBITS, 16cm tall.

DIRECTIONS:
Cut out patches adding 0.5cm seam allowance. Sew them together by machine.
FOR HORSE: Follow directions below.
FOR RABBITS: Make in same manner as HORSE. Make features.

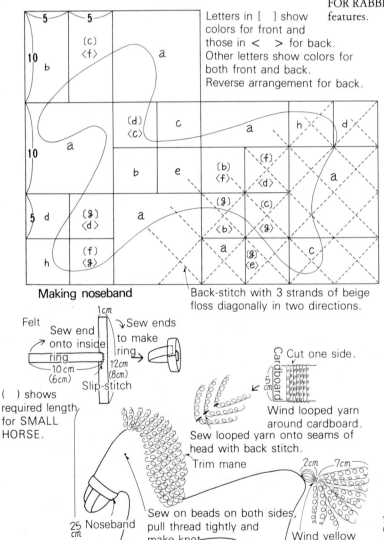

Letters in [ ] show colors for front and those in < > for back. Other letters show colors for both front and back. Reverse arrangement for back.

Back-stitch with 3 strands of beige floss diagonally in two directions.

Making noseband

Felt
Sew end onto inside ring
1cm
10cm (6cm)
Sew ends to make ring
12cm (8cm)
Slip-stitch

( ) shows required length for SMALL HORSE.

After piecing patches and finishing embroidery, cut out pattern adding 1cm seam allowance.
1cm
Pattern

With right sides of front and back together, stitch all around twice, leaving opening for turning. Trim excess 0.7cm beyond seams and clip into curves. Turn inside out. Stuff with polyester fiberfill and slip-stitch opening closed.

Making saddle

3.4
Red
Red with white dots
6.8
1.7
0.5
4.8
8.2
0.7
Slip-stitch

Sew patches together with 0.5cm seams.

Basting thread

Cut 7.2cm by 10.6cm from red for lining. Turn edges of lining over to turn in seam allowance and slip-stitch (see page 26).

Cut one side.
Cardboard 5cm
Wind looped yarn around cardboard.
Sew looped yarn onto seams of head with back stitch.
Trim mane

Sew on beads on both sides, pull thread tightly and make knot.

25cm Noseband

32cm

2cm 7cm
Wind yellow embroidery floss.

Slip-stitch saddle
5cm
2cm
Wind with red embroidery floss.
16cm
Sew on beads.
16cm

Cut strands of basting thread into 5cm pieces, place center of threads on seams of head and sew with back stitch.

GREEN RABBIT   Use fabric (a) for back.

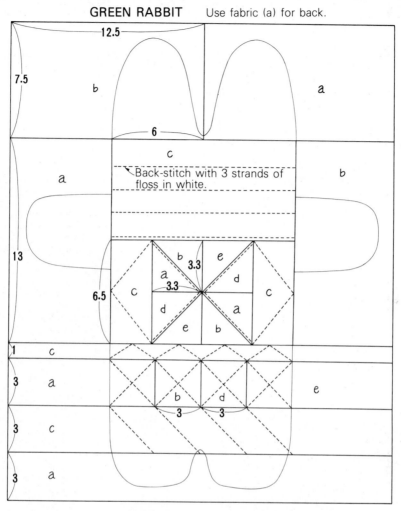

BLUE RABBIT Use blue for back.

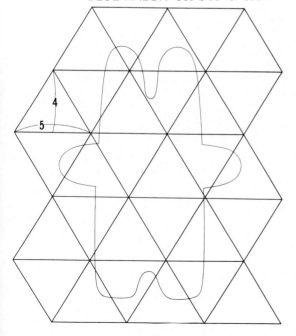

RED RABBIT Use red for back.

See page 87 for actual-size patterns.

X'MAS ORNAMENTS
Instructions for Pillows on page 91, for Wreath on page 34 and for other ornaments on page 114.

MATERIALS

FABRICS: Cotton fabric: (a) red with white dots, 50 cm by 15 cm; (b) print with large holly leaves, (c) red with design, 35 cm by 25 cm each; (d) print with small holly leaves 35 cm square; (e) red, 45 cm square. Green satin: 60 cm by 50 cm. Scrap of striped cotton for muffler. Six-strand embroidery floss, No. 25: White, gray, red and dark brown. Scraps of white and black felt. Red ribbon, 1.2 cm by 20 cm. Polyester fiberfill, 300 g. Black felt-tip pen.

FINISHED SIZE: 39 cm in diameter.

DIRECTIONS:

1. Cut out patches adding seam allowances. Sew them together by hand starting from center. Embroider.
2. Sew front and back together with right sides facing outside edge. Turn inside out.
3. Fold front seam allowance to back seam allowance of inside edge, and slip-stitch finely leaving opening for stuffing. Stuff with fiberfill tightly, and slip-stitch opening closed.
4. Sew loop for hanging onto back.
5. Tie ribbon into bow and sew on front.
6. Make snowman and attach in place.

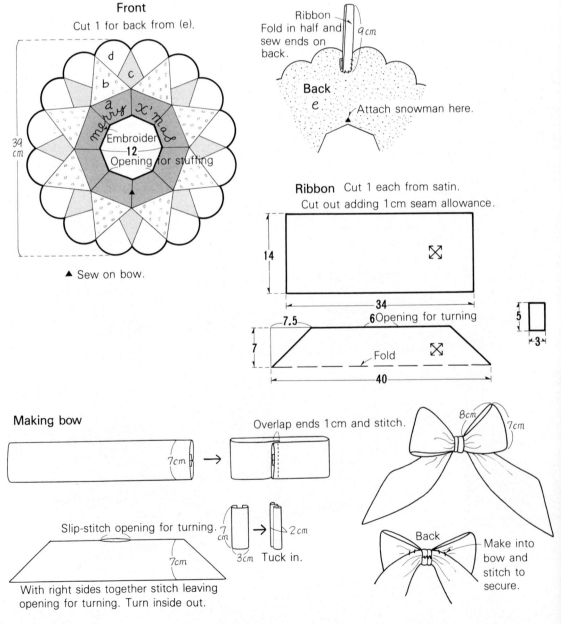

Patterns (Actual size)

Add 0.7 cm seam allowance.

$\frac{1}{8}$

Embroidery Pattern
Chain-stitch with 3 strands
of floss in white.

merry X'mas

d
Cut 16
↕

c
Cut 8
↕

b
Cut 8
↕

a
Cut 8
↕

Snowman

Opening for stuffing

No seam allowance on felt.

Head
Cut 2 in white.

Cap
Cut 2 in black.

Arm
Cut 2 in white

Opening for stuffing

Body
Cut 2 in white.

2.5 cm

Chain-stitch with 2 strands
of floss in gray.

Felt-tip pen

Straight-stitch with 2 strands
of floss in dark brown.

Fly-stitch with 4 strands
of floss in red.
Sew onto back.

9 cm

2 cm

Wind 4cm by 14cm
muffler around neck.
Overcast front and back
together leaving opening
for stuffing. Stuff with
fiberfill and overcast 35
opening closed.

See page 90 for Wreath with Santa Claus.

Lovely Patchwork

NORTH CAROLINA LILY WALL HANGING
Instructions on page 39.

MATERIALS

FABRIC: Cotton fabric: Small amount each for patches and appliques (see photo). Polyester fiberfill. White frame, 12.5cm (inside measurements). Cardboard, 13.2cm square. Star-shaped green spangles (medium) and transparent beads, 4 each for Yellow Heart. Star-shaped spangles (small), 5 blue & 4 silver; 9 transparent beads for Blue-Gray Heart. Star-shaped red spangles (medium) and transparent beads, 4 each for Red Heart.

FINISHED SIZE: Same size as frame.

DIRECTIONS:

1. Cut out patches and sew them together by hand.
2. Appliqué hearts, padding with fiberfill. Sew on spangles with beads.
3. Place fiberfill thinly over cardboard. Place pieced top over fiberfill and turn back seam allowance. Fix fabric with Scotch tape.
4. Frame.

Add 0.7cm seam allowance for piecing.
Add 2cm seam allowances to edges to be framed.

Appliqué patterns (Actual size)

Add 0.7cm seam allowance.
Pad with fiberfill and appliqué in slip stitch.

Yellow Heart ....Yellow
Blue-Gray Heart ... Blue-Gray
Red Heart ... Red
Cut 4 each

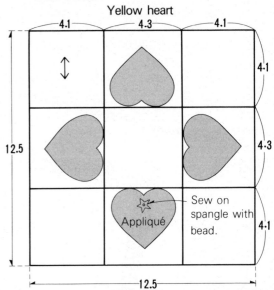

Yellow heart

Sew on spangle with bead.

Appliqué

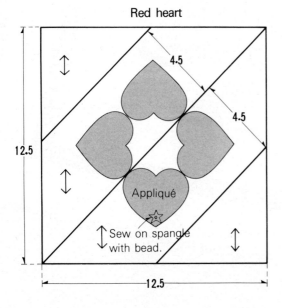

Red heart

Appliqué

Sew on spangle with bead.

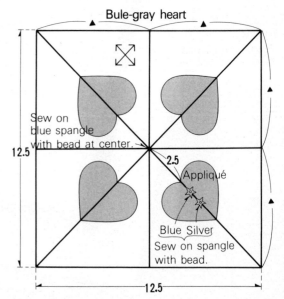

Bule-gray heart

Sew on blue spangle with bead at center.

Appliqué

Blue Silver
Sew on spangle with bead.

North Carolina Lily Wall Hanging,
shown on page 37.

MATERIALS

FABRICS: Sheeting: (a) white, 90cm by 130cm; (c) green, 35cm by 15cm; (f) navy, 90cm by 30cm. Floral prints: (b) 30cm by 15cm; (d, e) 15cm by 20cm each. Thin quilt batting, 70cm square. Quilting thread in white, navy and green.

FINISHED SIZE: 70cm square.

DIRECTIONS:

1. Cut out patches. Appliqué stems and handles in place. Then sew patches together by hand.
2. Transfer quilting patterns onto pieced top. Pin and baste top, batting and lining together.
3. Quilt along seams of patches with matching quilting thread. Then quilt birds and border patterns.
4. Bind edges to finish.

Piecing   Sew patches in numerical order.

Cutting

Top piece
    Add 0.7cm seam allowance.

	7cm × 68cm	Cut 2
	7cm × 54cm	Cut 2
	24cm triangle	Cut 4
a	12cm 〃	Cut 2
	10cm 〃	Cut 1
	24cm × 5cm	Cut 2
	12cm × 10cm	Cut 1
b	17cm triangle	Cut 1
	5cm 〃	Cut 2
f	3cm × 48cm	Cut 2
	3cm × 54cm	Cut 2

See patterns for flowers.
Cut batting 70cm square.
Lining Cut 1 70cm square
        for lining from (a).

Strip for binding

See page 18 for mitered corner.

Actual-size patterns are on page 93.

CRIB QUILTS

Duck Quilt Instructions on page 101.
Baby Quilt Instructions on page 42.

Baby Quilt, shown on page 41.

MATERIALS

FABRICS: Yellow and white gingham checks, 73 cm by 243 cm. Cotton broadcloth: Unbleached and white, 71 cm square each; yellow, 60 cm by 30 cm; small amount for appliques. Thick quilt batting, 120 cm by 90 cm. Quilt batting, 120 cm by 30 cm. White quilting thread. White cotton lace edging: 3.5 cm by 40 cm; 2.5 cm by 80 cm. One pink button, 1.7 cm in diameter. Six-strand embroidery floss, No. 25: Pink, light pink, yellow green, dark yellow green, light olive green, blue, light blue, gray and peony rose.

FINISHED SIZE: 118.5 cm by 86 cm.

DIRECTIONS:

1. Cut out patches and sew 6 squares together by machine.
2. Place smaller patches (a-c) and batting on pieced top and sew on in slip stitch.
3. Sew border strips around top piece.
4. With right sides facing, sew lining and top together, leaving opening for turning. Turn inside out. Insert batting and slip-stitch opening closed.
5. Quilt along seams. Appliqué from 1 to 6.

Cutting

Top piece … Add 1.5 cm seam allowance.
Cut 3 pieces each of 32.5 cm square from unbleached and white cotton broadcloth. Cut 4 pieces from gingham checks for border. See patterns for a-c.

Batting
Cut 118.5 cm by 86 cm
from thick quilt batting.

Lining
Cut 2 pieces of 121.5 cm by 46 cm from gingham checks and sew them together with 1.5 cm seams to make 121.5 cm by 89 cm. Sew 40 cm from each side leaving center open for turning.

Yellow cotton broadcloth …
Add 1 cm seam allowance.
Batting …
No seam allowance.

Appliqué patterns   Add 0.8cm seam allowance for fabric. No seam allowance for batting. Place appliqués at center of each square and sew in slip stitch catching lining.

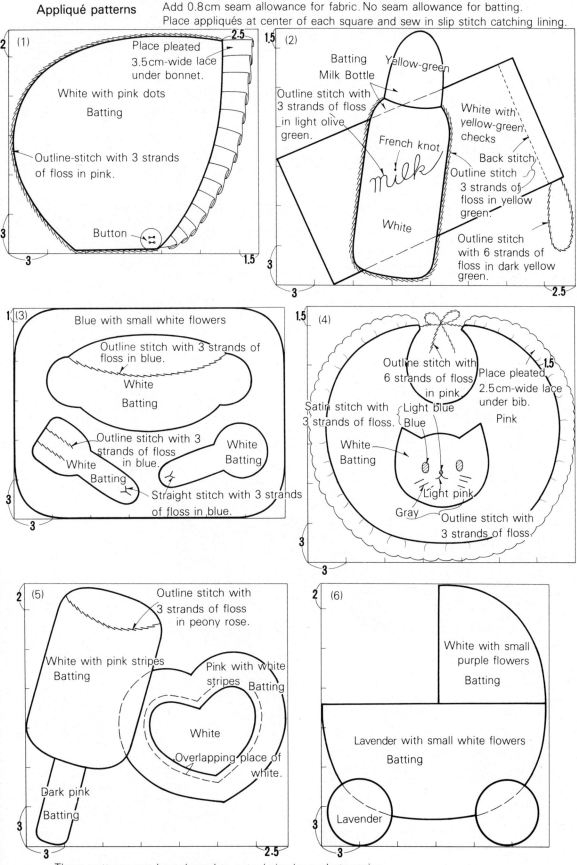

(1)
2
2.5
1.5
Place pleated
3.5cm-wide lace
under bonnet.
White with pink dots
Batting
Outline-stitch with 3 strands
of floss in pink.
3
Button
3
1.5

(2)
1.5
Batting   Yellow-green
Milk Bottle
Outline stitch with
3 strands of floss
in light olive
green.
French knot
milk
White
White with
yellow-green
checks
Back stitch
Outline stitch
3 strands of
floss in yellow
green.
Outline stitch
with 6 strands of
floss in dark yellow
green.
3
3
2.5

(3)
1
Blue with small white flowers
Outline stitch with 3 strands of
floss in blue.
White
Batting
Outline stitch with 3
strands of floss
in blue.
White
Batting
White
Batting
Straight stitch with 3 strands
of floss in blue.
3
3

(4)
1.5
Outline stitch with
6 strands of floss
in pink.
Place pleated
2.5cm-wide lace
under bib.
1.5
Satin stitch with
3 strands of floss.
Light blue
Blue
White
Batting
Pink
Light pink
Gray
Outline stitch with
3 strands of floss.
3

(5)
2
Outline stitch with
3 strands of floss
in peony rose.
White with pink stripes
Batting
Pink with white
stripes
Batting
White
Overlapping place of
white.
Dark pink
Batting
3
3
2.5

(6)
2
White with small
purple flowers
Batting
Lavender with small white flowers
Batting
Lavender
3
3

These patterns can be enlarged to actual size by a photocopier.

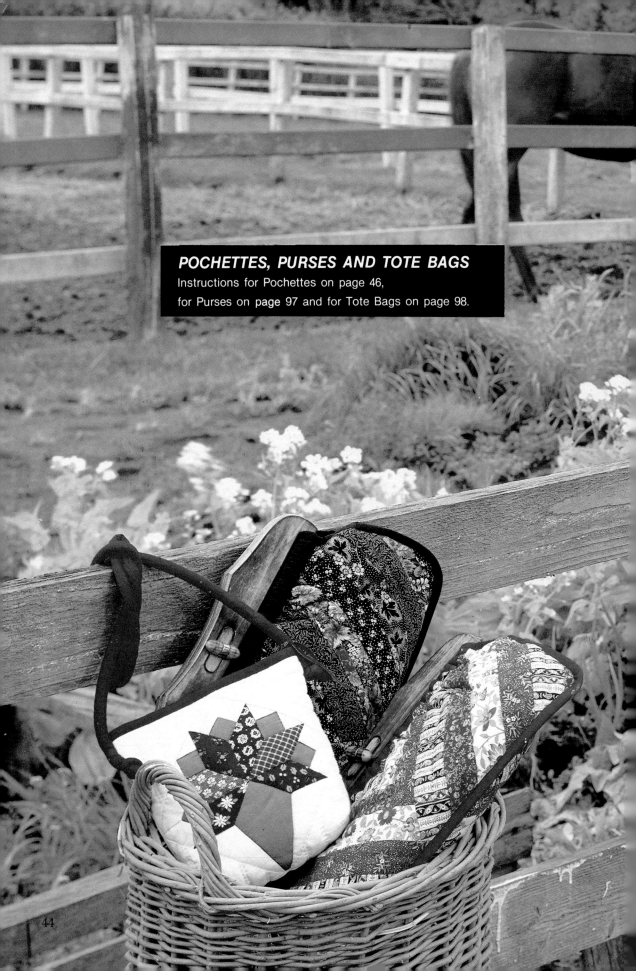

POCHETTES, PURSES AND TOTE BAGS
Instructions for Pochettes on page 46,
for Purses on page 97 and for Tote Bags on page 98.

CORNUCOPIA
MATERIALS
FABRICS: Cotton fabric: Red, 90 cm square; white, 50 cm by 25 cm; sage green, small amount; 6 different prints in tints of red, small amount each; for backing, 42 cm by 22 cm; for lining, 32 cm by 42 cm. Quilt batting, 42 cm by 22 cm. Outing flannel, 120 cm by 5 cm. White quilting thread. 20 cm zipper. Red leather string, 20 cm.
FINISHED SIZE: See diagram.

DIRECTIONS:
1. Cut out patches adding 0.7 cm seam allowance. Add 1 cm seam allowance to two sides of triangle. Sew patches together by hand.
2. Sew bottoms of front and back together. Draw quilting lines. Pin and baste top, batting and backing together. Quilt.
3. Make shoulder strap and strap holders.

4. With right sides facing and strap holders in between, sew side seams of front and back catching holders. Sew corners of bottom for gusset.
5. Sew inside pocket onto lining. Sew side seams and corners of bottom.
6. Insert lining into bag with wrong sides together. Sew on zipper.
7. Insert end of strap into holder and tie end.

Patterns (Actual size)

Add 0.7 cm seam allowance.

Cut 4 in white.

Cut 5 in sage green

White Cut 3 pairs (reverse pattern).

Cut 6 from prints.

White Cut 1 pair (reverse pattern)

Cut 1 in sage green.

( ) shows seam allowance.
Cut batting, backing and lining same size as top piece.
(Add 1 cm seam allowance) 0.5 2

2.5 Place for appliqué.

18

Front

Cream

36

Bottom Quilting White

Back

18

20

FLOWER
MATERIALS
FABRICS: Cotton fabric: Mustard, 90 cm square; cream, 38 cm by 22 cm; 9 different floral prints, small amount each; for backing, 38 cm by 22 cm; for lining, 33 cm by 38 cm. Quilt batting, 38 cm by 22 cm. Outing flannel, 120 cm by 6 cm. White and navy quilting thread. One 5 cm bamboo button.
FINISHED SIZE: See diagram.
DIRECTIONS:
1. Draw quilting lines and mark place for appliques. Cut out appliques and appliqué in place.
2. Pin and baste appliquéd piece, batting and backing together. Quilt.
3. Make shoulder strap and strap holders in same manner as CORNUCOPIA. Make button loop and button holder.
4. Fold in half with right sides together, sew side seams catching strap holders. Sew corners of bottom.
5. Sew lining as for CORNUCOPIA. Sew on inside pocket. Sew side seams and corners of bottom.
6. Bind edges for opening as shown on page 96.
7. Insert end of strap into holder and tie end.

Button loop

(No seam allowance) **Button holder**

5 Mustard

3

13

10

Cut shoulder strap, strip for binding and strap holder in same manner as CORNUCOPIA.
See opposite page for inside pocket.

(Continue to page 96)

Brighten Up the Kitchen

A: PLACEMAT B: NAPKIN C: CENTERPIECE D: TEA COZY E: MAT

Instructions for A & B on page 50, for C on page 51 and for D & E on page 99.

A: Placemat, shown on pages 48 & 49.

MATERIALS (FOR ONE)
FABRIC: Cotton fabric: (a) stripes, 26 cm square; (b) dots, 35 cm by 25 cm; (c) floral prints, 15 cm by 10 cm; (d) large checks, 23 cm by 12 cm; (e) small checks, 50.5 cm by 37 cm.
FINISHED SIZE: 44.5 cm by 31 cm.

DIRECTIONS:
Cut out patches adding 0.7 cm seam allowance. Sew them together by hand. Place top on lining with wrong sides together. Turn lining over top, turn in seam allowance and slip-stitch.

How to finish seam allowance
Turn in seam allowance and slip-stitch.

Turn lining over top.

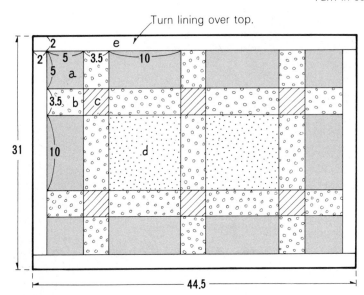

Cutting (For one)
Top piece Add 0.7 cm seam allowance

a	5 cm square	Cut 4
	5 cm × 10 cm	Cut 6
b	3.5 cm × 10 cm	Cut 7
	3.5 cm × 5 cm	Cut 10
c	3.5 cm square	Cut 6
d	10 cm square	Cut 2

Lining   Cut out 50.5 cm by 37 cm from (e)

B: Napkins, shown on pages 48 & 49.

MATERIALS (FOR ONE)
FABRIC: Cotton fabric: (e) small checks, 54 cm by 50 cm; (a) stripes, (b) dots, (c) floral prints, small amount each.
FINISHED SIZE: 52 cm by 48 cm.
DIRECTIONS:
Cut fabric adding seam allowance. Appliqué in place. Fold edges twice and machine-stitch.

Add 1 cm seam allowance.

Finishing

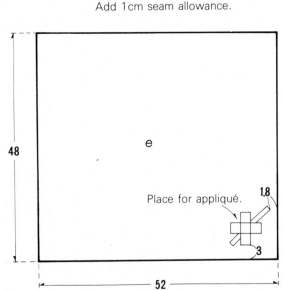

Fold twice and machine stitch.

Place for appliqué.

Appliqué patterns
(Actual size)

Add 0.3cm seam allowance for a, and 0.7cm seam allowance for b, c.

 C: Centerpiece, shown on pages 48 & 49.

MATERIALS
FABRIC: Cotton fabric. (a-i) small amount each of 9 different prints for patches; for lining, small checks, 38cm by 25cm.
FINISHED SIZE: 34cm by 21cm.

DIRECTIONS:
Cut out patches and sew them together by hand. Place pieced top on lining with wrong sides together. Turn lining over top, turn in seam allowance and slip-stitch.

Cut out for lining adding 2cm seam allowance in checks.

Turn lining over top.

Check

6.3

3.6

1.5

21

34

Finishing

Fold twice in numerical order, and slip-stitch.

1.5cm ②   ①   Fix lining with thread at intervals.

③

Patterns (Actual size)
Add 0.7cm seam allowance.

Cut 30

Cut 8
Cut 4 (reverse pattern)

KITCHEN ACCESSORIES

Toaster Oven Cover Instructions on page 119.
Electric Cooker Cover Instructions on page 117.
Pot Holders Instructions on page 54.

Pot Holders, shown on pages 52 & 53.

ANVIL, shown at left
MATERIALS
FABRICS: Cotton fabric: Beige, 35 cm by 20 cm; dark brown with white dots, 18 cm by 28 cm; brown and white stripes, 17 cm square; small amount of brick red; lining, 17 cm square. Outing flannel, 34 cm by 17 cm. White quilting thread.
FINISHED SIZE: 17 cm square.

DIRECTIONS:
1. Cut out patches and sew them together by hand.
2. Pin and baste pieced top, outing flannel and lining together. Quilt along 0.5 cm inside of each patch.
3. Pin and baste back piece, outing flannel and lining together. Quilt diagonally in two directions at 2.5 cm intervals.
4. Pin and baste front and back together with wrong sides facing. Bind edges to finish, catching ends of hanging loop in place.

Front

Top piece (patchwork) See patterns.
Cut 17 cm square each from
outing flannel and lining.

0.5
Quilting
15
15

Back

Cut 17 cm square each from
top piece (beige) and outing flannel.

2.5
2.5
Quilting
17
17

Strips for binding

Cut 4 in dark brown
with white dots
4
18

Hanging loop

Dark brown with
white dots
4
8

Hanging loop 1cm
Turn in seam allowances and machine-stitch.

Back

3 cm
Fold strip in
half, insert
ends of loop
under binding
and slip-stitch.

Overcast
securely
1 cm width binding

Turn in end
17 cm
17 cm

Patterns (Actual size)

Add 0.7 cm seam allowance.

Cut 10 in beige
Cut 2 in brick

Cut 2 in beige.

Stripe
Cut 2 each
reversing pattern.

Cut 2 in dark brown
in white dots.

54

DUTCH MILL, shown at right
MATERIALS
FABRICS: Cotton fabric: Red with small flowers, 25 cm by 20 cm; green, 18 cm by 21 cm; unbleached, 25 cm by 15 cm; small amount each of floral prints with white, yellow and blue background; for lining, 17 cm square. Outing flannel, 34 cm by 17 cm. White quilting thread.

FINISHED SIZE: 17 cm square.
DIRECTIONS: Make in same manner as ANVIL.

Front

Top piece (patchwork) See patterns.

Cut 17 cm square each from outing flannel and lining.

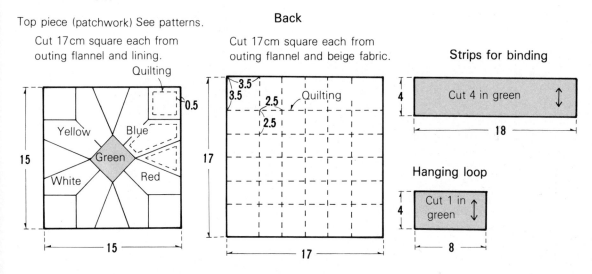

Back

Cut 17 cm square each from outing flannel and beige fabric.

Strips for binding

Cut 4 in green
18

Hanging loop

Cut 1 in green
4
8

Hanging loop

Fold strip in half, and sew.

Turn in seam allowances, and machine-stitch.

1 cm width binding

Turn in end

Patterns (Actual size)

Add 0.7 cm seam allowance.

Cut 4 in unbleached
Cut 1 in green

Cut 1 each (reverse pattern) in print fabric ...
Cut 8

Cut 4 in unbleached

OCTAGON potholder is on page 102 and MITTEN on page 103.

COMFORTABLE BEDROOMS

CHURN DASH BEDSPREAD

Instructions on page 58.

Fabrics Used (Actual Size)

Churn Dash Bedspread,
shown on pages 56 & 57.

MATERIALS

FABRICS: Cotton fabric: (a) 90cm by 260cm; (b) 90cm by 140cm; (c) 90cm by130cm; (d) 90cm by 95cm; (e) 90cm by 65cm; (f, g) 90cm by 30cm each; (h) 50cm by 20cm; (i) 90cm square; (j) 90cm by 10cm; (k) 90cm by 80cm; (l) 90cm by 60cm; (m) 90cm by 30cm; (n, o) 90cm by 20cm each; (p) 90cm by 40cm; (q) 20cm by 15cm. Sheeting for lining, 91cm by 490cm. Quilt batting, 92cm by 5m. White quilting thread.
FINISHED SIZE: 244.5cm by 181.5cm.

DIRECTIONS:

1. Cut out patches and sew them together by hand. Make required pieces of 7 different blocks. Join 10 by blocks.
2. Sew border (b) & (c) to pieced blocks. Transfer quilting patterns to (c).
3. Sew pieces of batting and lining together.
4. Pin and baste pieced top, batting and lining together. Quilt along inside of center patches and diagonal lines of each block starting from center.
5. Bind edges with (a) and quilt at corners, along seams and folded edges.

Cutting

Top piece

Add 0.7cm seam allowance.

See next page for blocks 1 to 7.

a	3.5cm×17.5cm	Cut 79
	3.5cm square	Cut 48
b	1.5cm×70cm	Cut 2
	1.5cm×94.5cm	″
	1.5cm×96cm	″
	1.5cm×134.5cm	″
c	7cm×70cm	″
	7cm×94.5cm	″
	7cm×87.5cm	″
	7cm×126cm	″
d	3.5cm×17.5cm	Cut 78
e	3.5cm square	Cut 40

Batting

Place 2 pieces of 92cm by 247cm side by side and overcast to make one piece 184cm by 247cm.

Lining

Sew 2 pieces of 91cm by 244.5cm side by side and overcast to make 181.5cm by 244.5cm.

Border strip

Add 0.7cm seam allowance.

78.5 = Cut 2
103 = Cut 4
141.5 = Cut 2

Motif

Add 0.7 cm seam allowance.

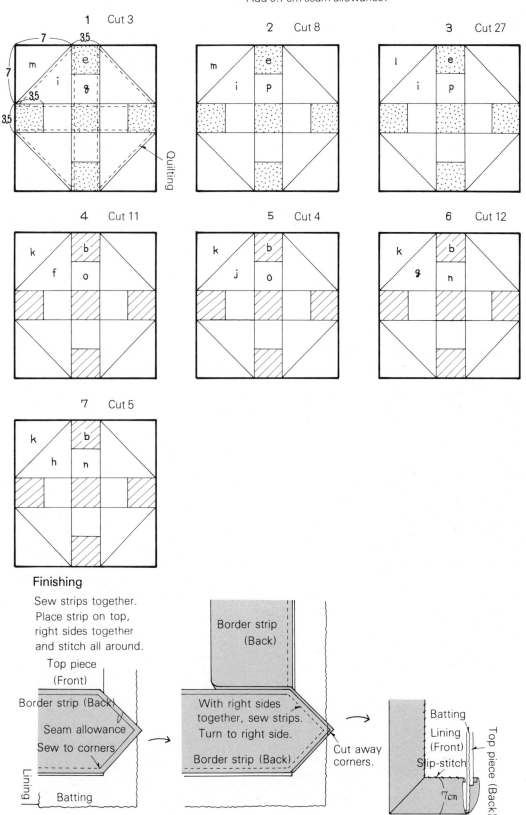

1   Cut 3

7
3,5
7
m
e
i
g
3,5
3,5
Quilting

2   Cut 8

m
e
i
p

3   Cut 27

l
e
i
p

4   Cut 11

k
b
f
o

5   Cut 4

k
b
j
o

6   Cut 12

k
b
g
n

7   Cut 5

k
b
h
n

Finishing

Sew strips together.
Place strip on top,
right sides together
and stitch all around.

Top piece
(Front)

Border strip (Back)

Seam allowance
Sew to corners

Lining

Batting

Border strip
(Back)

With right sides
together, sew strips.
Turn to right side.

Border strip (Back)

Cut away
corners.

Batting

Lining
(Front)

Slip-stitch

Top piece (Back)

7 cm

Quilting patterns are on page 106.

59

Fabrics Used
(Actual Size)
For Muffler

a
b
c
d

QUILTED HAPPI COATS FOR MOTHER AND CHILD
Instructions for Happi Coat for Mother on page 62,
for Child on page 106 and for Muffler on page 105.

Fabrics Used (Actual Size)
For Mother

a
b
c
d
e

Fabrics Used (Actual Size) For Child

61

Quilted Happi Coat for Mother,
shown on pages 60 & 61.

MATERIALS
FABRICS: Cotton fabric: (e) navy, 90 cm by 320 cm; (a-d) 30 cm by 15 cm each. Fabrics for backing and lining, 90 cm by 280 cm each. Quilt batting, 70 cm by 280 cm. Thin quilt batting for pocket, 42 cm by 21 cm. White quilting thread.

FINISHED SIZE: Width across back, 64 cm. Length, 69.5 cm. Sleeve length from center back, 63 cm.
DIRECTIONS:
1. Cut out left and right pieces following diagram.
2. Cut out patches and sew them together by hand.

Cut out left piece (reverse pattern).
Cut batting, backing and lining same size as top piece.

Strips for binding

Pocket Cut two pieces 21 cm
Left and right pieces = 285 cm

Piecing

Right piece   Left piece

Pocket

Cut thin quilt batting, backing and lining same size as top piece.

3. Sew patches onto left and right pieces in slip stitch.
4. Sew back seams of top, backing and lining individually and press seams open. Overlap 3 cm at center back of batting and sew with large stitches.
5. Mark quilting lines on top.
6. Pin and baste top, batting and backing together. Quilt along quilting lines and outside of patches.
7. Sew patches to pocket pieces. Mark quilting lines.
8. Pin and baste top, batting and backing together and quilt in same way as body.

9. Place lining of pocket on quilted piece. Bind top edges, sew onto body in blind stitch and top-stitch.
10. Sew side and sleeve seams. Press seams open. Make lining in same manner. Insert lining into top and sew sleeve seams of backing and lining together by hand.
11. Turn in seam allowances of sleeve lining 0.5 cm in from sleeve opening and slip-stitch. Fix lining with back stitch.
12. Bind front and bottom edges to finish.

Patterns (Actual size)
Add 0.7 cm seam allowance.

a ~ d Cut 10 each
e Cut 40

a ~ d Cut 5 each

Piecing

Stitch between marks
(don't stitch across seam allowances.)

(1) Sew 3 printed patches (shaded area) together and press seams toward center.
(2) Sew on solids and press seams to print side.
(3) Sew blocks together. Press seams to print side.

→ shows direction for turning seams.

Place lining 0.5 cm in from sleeve opening and slip-stitch. Back-stitch 0.5 cm from slip-stitch.

57 cm

12 cm

Sew patches onto top in slip-stitch.

Sew seams of top and lining together to fix.

1 cm wide binding 7.5 cm

Top-stitch 1 cm in from edge.

Sew on pocket in blind stitch. 1 cm wide binding

4 cm

See page 18 for mitered corner.

See page 106 for Child's Happi Coat.

63

HOUSE AND TREE BEDSPREAD

Instructions on page 66.

*Fabrics Used
(Actual Size)*

a
b
c
d
e
f
g
h
i
j
k
l
m
n
o
p

House and Tree Bedspread,
shown on pages 64 & 65.

MATERIALS
FABRICS: Coton fabric: (a) 90 cm by 360 cm; (b) 90 cm by 280 cm; (c) 90 cm by 25 cm; (d) 50 cm by 25 cm; (e) 40 cm by 20 cm; (f) 90 cm by 45 cm; (g) 30 cm by 20 cm; (h) 90 cm by 50 cm; (i) 30 cm by 20 cm; (j) 60 cm by 25 cm; (k) 90 cm by 15 cm; (l,m) small amount each; (n) 40 cm by 20 cm; (o) 35 cm by 15 cm; (p) 50 cm by 20 cm. Quilted fabric for lining, 86 cm by 452 cm. Six-strand embroidery floss, No. 25: Powder green, brown and pink.

FINISHED SIZE: 170 cm by 226 cm.
DIRECTIONS:
1. Cut out required number of squares and border strips. Enlarge appliqué patterns and cut out appliques.
2. Appliqué onto each square following diagram. Place clouds and other appliques from 2 to 7 as indicated matching centers.
3. Machine-stitch 7 squares together in rows with short strips (b) in between, then sew them together with long strips (b) in between.
4. Sew pieces of lining together.
5. Place top on lining with wrong sides facing and sew together with two rows of machine-stitiching.
6. Sew border to top.

Cutting
Top piece
Add 1 cm seam allowance.
a......Cut 35 pieces of
     28 cm square.
b......Cut 30 pieces of
     5 cm by 28 cm.
     Cut 4 pieces of
     5 cm by 216 cm.
Lining
   Sew 2 pieces of 86 cm by 226 cm together with 1 cm seams to make one piece 170 cm by 226 cm.

See page 2 for finishing corners.

Border strip   Add 1 cm seam allowance.

216
170 Cut 2 each

Appliqué patterns

Cut 5
Add 0.7 cm seam allowance.
Embroider with 4 strands of floss.
Place on (a) and appliqué in slip stitch.

3.3

h

3

3   3.3

2.3 Cut 5 each
[   ] shows 3.

2.5

f
[i]

P
[g]

f
[j]

Center
1.5

k k k

3

3   1   2
Center

4 Cut 5

1.5

k   k

c

Center
2

j

o

n   n

h

e

3

k

n   n

n

3   1.5
Center

5 Cut 5

1.5

h

Center

h

3

3   2   1
Center

6 Cut 5

1.5

d

c

e

Outline stitch
in powder
green.

Center
1.5

j   j   f   f

f   f

3

3
Center

7 Cut 5

2.5

e

Straight
stitch

Brown
Pink

l   l

m

Outline stitch
Brown Powder green

n

n   n

f   f

m   m   f

f

k

f

d

f

f

Center

c

f   f

3

o   o

3   1.2   3.3
Center

These patterns can be enlarged to actual size by a photocopier.

67

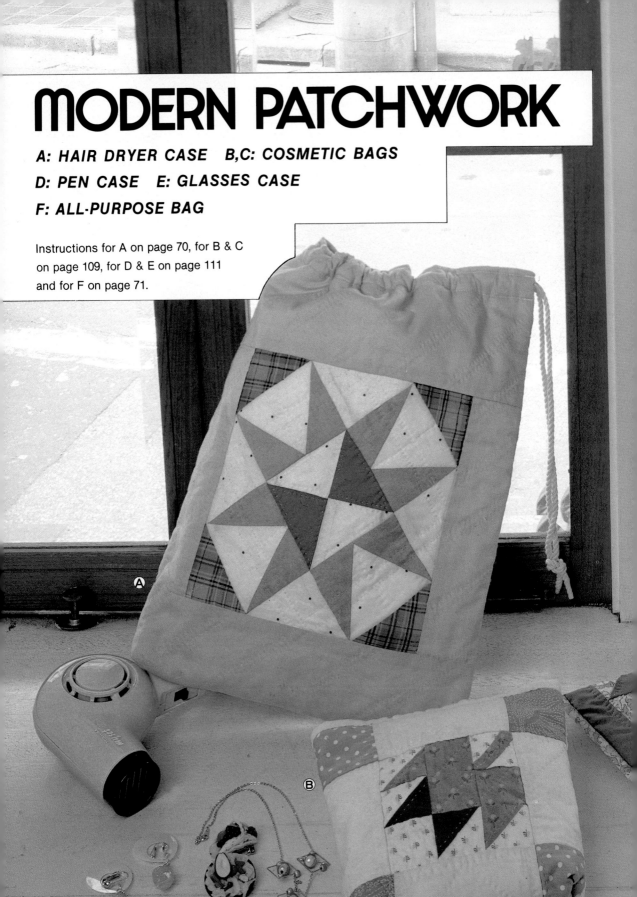

MODERN PATCHWORK

A: HAIR DRYER CASE   B,C: COSMETIC BAGS
D: PEN CASE   E: GLASSES CASE
F: ALL-PURPOSE BAG

Instructions for A on page 70, for B & C on page 109, for D & E on page 111 and for F on page 71.

A: Hair Dryer Case,
shown on pages 68 & 69.

MATERIALS

FABRIC: Cotton fabric: (a) powder green, 60cm by 45cm; (b-e) 4 different prints (see photo) for patches, small amount each; for lining, 60cm by 40cm. Quilt batting, 60cm by 40cm. White quilting thread. Cotton cord, 0.5cm in diameter and 95cm long.

FINISHED SIZE: See diagram.

DIRECTIONS:

1. Cut out patches adding seam allowance. Sew them together by hand. Sew center block and fabric (a).
2. Mark quilting lines on pieced front and back. Pin and baste front and batting together. Quilt. Quilt back in same way.
3. Sew front and back together with right sides facing. Sew corners at bottom. Turn inside out.
4. Make lining in same way.
5. Insert lining into quilted bag with wrong sides together. Turn in seam allowances and slip stitch at each side. Fold top edges and stitch to make casing.
6. Insert cotton cord into casing.

(　　) shows seam allowance.
Add 1cm seam allowance unless otherwise indicated.
Cut 2 pieces for quilt batting, 30cm by 40cm each.
Cut 2 pieces for lining, 29.5cm by 40cm each.

Patterns (Actual size)　　　Add 0.7cm seam allowance.

How to make casing

Top piece (Wrong side)

5cm

33cm

24cm

Quilt batting

Opening end

9cm

Overlap lining on Top piece

Slip stich 0.2cm in from edge.

Lining (Right side)

Gusset

2cm
4cm

Machine stitch

Casing

0.5cm
Machine stitch
0.5cm

3cm

F: All-purpose Bag, shown on pages 68 & 69.

MATERIALS
FABRIC: Cotton fabric: Off-white, 60cm by 25cm; 9 different prints (see photo) for patches, small amount each; for lining, 50cm by 26cm. Quilt batting, 50cm by 26cm. White quilting thread. One button, 1.8cm in diameter.
FINISHED SIZE: See diagram.
DIRECTIONS:
1. Cut out patches and sew 3 strips together to make square. Make 18 squares and join 3 by 3 squares.

2. Sew bottom seams of front and back together. Mark quilting lines. Pin and baste top and batting together. Quilt.
3. Sew side seams with right sides together. Turn inside out.
4. Make lining in same way. Make button loop.
5. Insert lining into quilted bag with wrong sides together and bind top edges catching ends of button loop.
6. Sew on button.

Add 0.7cm seam allowance.

8
8

Off-white

Front, Back
Cut 1 each

Quilting

24

Lining
Quilt batting } Cut 1 each

Fold

24

24

Button loop

0.5cm
Fold strip twice, and slip stitch.

Bind top edges catching ends of button loop.

Binding, 0.7cm wide

Button

24.7 cm

24cm

Strip for binding

2.8 ⊤₁ Off-white ↕
50

Button loop

2 ⊤₁ ↕ Off-white
10

A: SEWING BOX   B,C,D,E,F: PINCUSHIONS
G: SCISSORS CASE   H: TELEPHONE   COVER

Instructions for A on page 120, for B—E on page 74, for F on page 121,
for G on page 113 and for H on page 123.

72

FOR B
MATERIALS
FABRIC: Cotton broadcloth: small amount each of pink and soft pink floral prints. Quilt batting, 6 cm square. Pink embroidery floss, No. 25. White cotton lace edging, 1 cm by 35 cm. Cotton for stuffing.
FINISHED SIZE: 10 cm in diameter.
DIRECTIONS:
1. Cut out patches adding seam allowance. Sew prints and solids together alternately by hand.
2. Pin and baste soft pink fabric and batting together. Quilt. Place quilted piece on center of patches and slip-stitch.
3. Cut out back piece. With right sides facing, sew front and back together leaving opening for stuffing. Turn inside out. Stuff with cotton and slip-stitch opening closed.

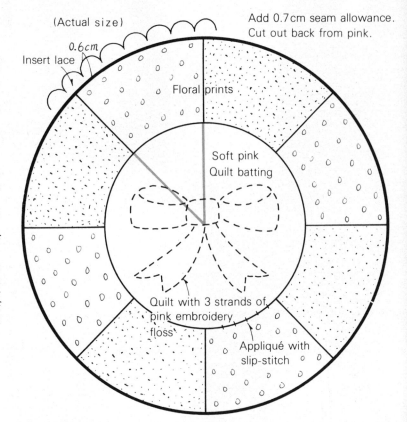

(Actual size)

Add 0.7 cm seam allowance.
Cut out back from pink.

0.6 cm
Insert lace

Floral prints

Soft pink
Quilt batting

Quilt with 3 strands of pink embroidery floss

Appliqué with slip-stitch

(Actual size) Add 0.7 cm seam allowance.
Cut out back piece in blue.

Insert lace between patches and back piece
0.6 cm

Sew ribbon onto patches.
Floral prints

FOR C
MATERIALS
FABRIC: 8 different floral prints; small amount of blue cotton broadcloth. Blue satin ribbon, 0.9 cm by 35 cm. white cotton lace edging, 1 cm by 45 cm. Cotton for stuffing.
FINISHED SIZE: One side of octagon, 4 cm.
DIRECTIONS:
1. Cut out patches adding seam allowance. Sew ribbon onto 4 triangles. Sew triangles together by hand.
2. Make in same way as B.

FOR D
MATERIALS
FABRIC: Cotton broadcloth:
Small amount each of pink,
orange and 5 different prints.
Red bias tape, 1.8cm by 42cm.
Cotton for stuffing.
FINISHED SIZE: About 11cm
square.
DIRECTIONS:
1. Cut out patches adding seam
   allowance and sew them
   together by hand.
2. Cut out back piece. With wrong
   sides facing, sew front and back
   together leaving opening for
   stuffing. Stuff with cotton and
   slip-stitch opening closed.
3. Bind edges with bias tape.

(Actual size)

Add 0.7cm seam allowance for sewing together,
and 0.9cm seam allowance for edges.
Cut out back piece in pink.

With wrong sides of front
and back facing,
sew along seam line.

Seam allowance

Binding

Round corners

(Actual size)

FOR E
MATERIALS
FABRIC: Cotton broadcloth: Small
amount each of blue, pink, light
green and yellow. Quilt batting,
11cm square. Bright yellow bias
tape, 1.8cm by 48cm White
quilting thread. Cotton for
stuffing.
FINISHED SIZE: about 11cm
square.
DIRECTIONS:
1. Cut out squares adding seam
   allowance and sew them
   together by hand.
2. Pin and baste top and batting
   together. Quilt.
3. Cut out back piece. Sew quilted
   front and back together with
   wrong sides facing leaving
   opening for stuffing. Stuff with
   cotton and slip-stitch opening
   closed.
4. Bind edges with bias tape.

Add 0.7cm seam allowance for sewing together,
and 0.9cm seam allowance for edges.
Cut out back piece in blue.

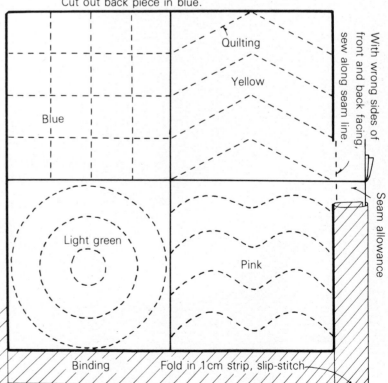

With wrong sides of
front and back facing,
sew along seam line.

Seam allowance

Binding   Fold in 1cm strip, slip-stitch

A: SHOE PADS
B: SHOE CASE
C,D: LIDS FOR BASKETS

Instructions for A & B on page 78, for C on page 79 and for D on page 108.

Fabrics Used
(Actual Size)

Shoe Pads and Shoe Case,
shown on pages 76 & 77.

FOR SHOE PADS
MATERIALS (FOR ONE PAIR)
FABRIC: Cotton fabric; salmon pink, 30 cm square; small amount each of pink, purple and green. Quilt batting, 25 cm by 15 cm. Green sewing thread. Polyester fiberfill.
FINISHED SIZE: See diagram.
DIRECTIONS:
1. Cut out patches and sew them together by machine.
2. Machine-stitch pieced front and batting together along seams.
3. Sew front and back together with right sides facing leaving top edge open. Turn inside out.
4. Make loop.
5. Stuff with fiberfill. Turn in seam allowances of top edges, insert ends of loop and sew opening closed. Pull thread and tie knot.

Patterns (Actual size)

Add 0.7 cm seam allowance.
Cut out 2 pieces each of lining (Salmon pink) and quilt batting same size as top piece.

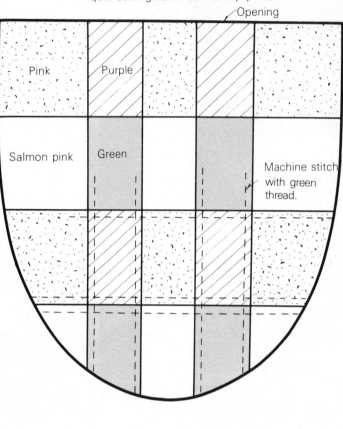

Opening

Pink

Purple

Salmon pink

Green

Machine stitch with green thread.

Turn in seam allowances of top edges, insert ends of loop and sew opening closed. Pull thread and tie knot.

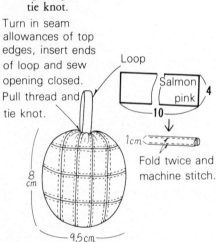

Loop

Salmon pink

4

10

1 cm

Fold twice and machine stitch.

8 cm

9.5 cm

FOR SHOE CASE
MATERIALS
FABRIC: Pink cotton fabric, 76 cm by 34 cm. Ribbon: 2.2 cm by 152 cm; 2 kinds, 1.4 cm by 76 cm; 2.4 cm by 76 cm and 2.6 cm by 76 cm. 2 pieces of pink cotton cord, 0.2 cm in diameter and 50 cm long each.
FINISHED SIZE: See diagram.
DIRECTIONS:
Sew ribbon onto pink fabric. Fold in half crosswise with right sides together and sew side and bottom seams. Fold seam allowance of opening and stitch. Sew on ribbon for casing. Insert cotton cord into casing.

Add 1 cm seam allowance.

1.8 cm

Casing

4

2.2

Opening end

32

Cut 2 in pink

Fold

Sew ribbon with machine stitch.

2.4
1.4
2.2
1.4
2.6

18

32 cm

18 cm

Detail of top edge

Fold top edge and stitch.
Then fold side edge and stitch.

a

b

Opening end

→

2 2cm Ribbon d Stitch

C Turn in
1cm and
stitch.

Opening end

Coiled Lid for Basket, shown on page 76.

MATERIALS
FABRIC: Cotton fabric: (a) 90cm by 40cm; (b-h) 90cm
by 7cm each. Cotton cord, 0.8cm in diameter and 11cm
long. Cardboard, 30cm in diameter.
FINISHED SIZE: 32cm in diameter.

DIRECTIONS:
Cut out strips and sew them together as indicated. Cover
cotton cord with pieced strip and slip-stitch. Coil and
overcast to fix following diagram. Make ties and sew on
wrong side. Run a gathering stitch around back piece,
cover cardboard and slip-stitch back to wrong side of coil-
ed front.

Making coil

Sew 89 strips together
with 0.5cm seams.
Press seams open.

Place cotton cord
at center.

Cover tightly and
slip-stitch.

Cutting strips and sewing together

Cut out strips 3.5cm wide (8 strips,
60cm long from a. 2 strips each, 90cm long from
b, c, d, e, f, g, h) and sew strips together 12
times in alphbetical order as indicated below.

time →

	First	2 ″	3·4 ″	5·6 ″	7·8 ″	9·10 ″	11 ″	12 ″
a	22cm	6cm	8cm	10cm	12cm	14cm	16cm	250cm
b	6 ″	6 ″	8 ″	10 ″	12 ″	14 ″	16 ″	
C	6 ″	6 ″	8 ″	10 ″	12 ″	14 ″	16 ″	
d	6 ″	6 ″	8 ″	10 ″	12 ″	14 ″	16 ″	
e	6 ″	6 ″	8 ″	10 ″	12 ″	14 ″	16 ″	
f	6 ″	6 ″	8 ″	10 ″	12 ″	14 ″	16 ″	
g	6 ″	6 ″	8 ″	10 ″	12 ″	14 ″	16 ″	
h	6 ″	6 ″	8 ″	10 ″	12 ″	14 ″	16 ″	

Add 1cm
seam allowance.

Bottom

Cut 1 piece from a.

30

Cord

3 ⅓

Cut 8 pieces from a.

25

Wrong side

Coil and
overcast
from center.

(It is easier to work if you
place covered cord on
working board
and pin centers
of coil)

Bring seams
to inside to
hide from front.

Cardboard

Slip-stitch
ends of 2 ties
onto wrong side
of coil.

Finally, slip-stitch coil
end to wrong side.

Slip-stitch
Run a
gathering
stitch

1cm

30cm

Cardboard
30cm in
diameter.

Turn inside out.
Turn in end and
slip-stitch.

After coiling 20
and a half rounds,
diameter will
be about 32cm.

8cm

23.5cm

Fold in half
lengthwise
with right
sides together
and stitch.

1cm

79

TISSUE BOX COVER

Instructions on page 81.

COVER WITH YO-YO FLOWERS
MATERIALS
FABRICS: Cotton broadcloth: Cream, 76cm by 16cm; salmon pink, 45cm by 20cm; powder green, 30cm square; pink, 20cm square. Outing flannel, 76cm by 16cm. Elastic tape, 2 pieces, 0.8cm by 14cm. Soft pink rickrack, 1cm by 77cm.

FINISHED SIZE: See diagram.

DIRECTIONS:
1. Cut out patches and machine- stitch together in numerical order.

2. Place pieced patches on outing flannel and machine-stitch along seams.
3. Sew side seams. Fold bottom edges and machine-stitch.
4. Make top following diagram. Sew top and side together with right sides facing and rickrack in between. Turn inside out.
5. Make yo-yo flowers and sew on top.
6. Sew elastic tape onto bottom.

81

LUNCH BOX TISSUE CASE

MATERIALS

FABRICS: Cotton broadcloth: Red, 90cm by 30cm; dark green, 30cm by 15cm; small amount each of green and cream. Outing flannel, 53cm by 31cm. Red embroidery floss, No. 25. Elastic tape, 2 pieces of 0.8cm by 10cm each. 2 red buttons, 1.5cm in diameter. Polyester fiberfill.

FINISHED SIZE: See diagram.

DIRECTIONS:

Make in numerical order from 1 to 8 following diagram. Stuff top part with fiberfill. (Adjust amount of fiberfill after covering tissue box.)

( ) shows seam allowance and add 0.5cm seam allowance unless otherwise indicated. Cut 1 piece each, 26.5cm by 31cm and 26.5cm by 7cm, from outing flannel.

Strip Red
Cut 2 for top edges, 25.5cm, and 1 for bottom, 71cm

Stay
Cut 2 in red
Cut 2 pieces, 4cm by 3cm, from outing flannel.

Handle Cut 1 in red
Cut 1 piece, 18cm by 2cm, from outing flannel.

Back
Side   Cut 1 in red
Front   Top edge

Gusset
Cut 2 pieces from outing flannel same size as top piece

Red
Dark Green   Green

Appliqué
Cut 1 in cream
(Add 1cm seam allowance all around)
Fold line
Embroidery
Lunch

Sew gussets to front and back matching marks

Embroidery patterns (Actual size)
Outline-stitch with 6 strands of red floss.

5. Embroider letters and appliqué in place.

6. Fold in same way as stay and machine-stitch all around. Sew on with button.

7. Sew gussets and lined front and back together.

2. Sew patches and gusset together (Sew the other side).

1. Machine-stitch patches together

Sew on stay.

3. Sew strip along edges
Outing flannel (Right side)
Strip (Wrong side)
Place pieced patches on outing flannel. Place strip on with right sides facing and stitch.

Turn in 1cm of strip and stitch. Sew strip onto other opening side in same way.

8. Sew strip along edges and bind in same way as top opening. Sew on elastic tape.
Strip (Wrong side)
Sew other end to opposite side.

4. Place outing flannel on wrong side of stay and fold as shown.
Fold line   Outing flannel

Continued from page 7

Quilting patterns   (Actual size)

Center

Continued from page 27

Appliqué patterns (Actual size)

Cut out one piece adding 0.5cm seam allowance.
Pad with cotton and appliqué in slip stich.
Work with 3 strands of embroidery thread.

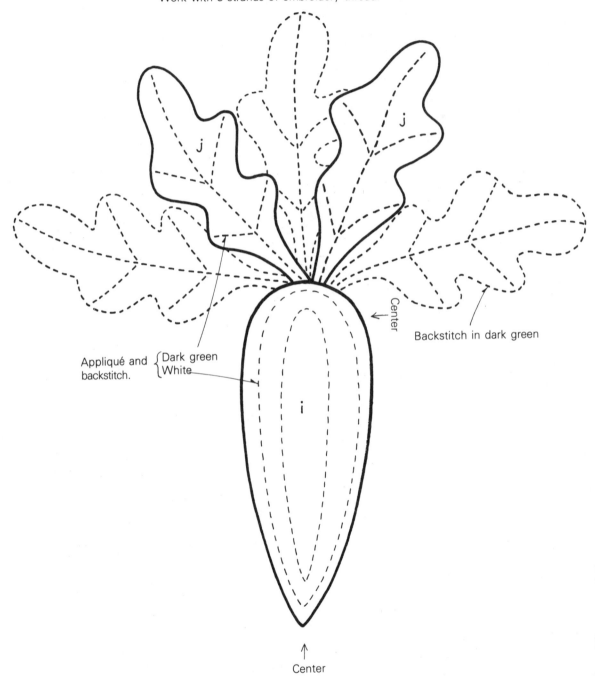

Center

Backstitch in dark green

Appliqué and
backstitch.
Dark green
White

i

↑
Center

Backstitch in green

Appliqué and backstitch in red.

k

Center

↑
Center

  House Wall Hanging, shown on page 28.

MATERIALS
FABRIC: Cotton fabric: (See photo for colors and designs.) (a) 58 cm square; (b) 90 cm by 28 cm; (c) 7 cm square; (d) 50 cm square; small amount each of 16 different solids and prints for appliques; for lining, 71 cm square. Quilt batting, 71 cm square. White quilting thread. Navy embroidery floss, No. 25.
FINISHED SIZE: 71 cm square.

DIRECTIONS:
1. Cut out patches and borders. Appliqué house onto each square in slip stitch. Embroider date and name.
2. Sew squares together with borders by machine.
3. Pin and baste top, batting and lining together and quilt.
4. Bind edges to finish.

Appliqué patterns

(Actual size)

Add 0.7cm seam allowance.

Quilting

Cutting

Top piece Add 1cm seam allowance.

a	27cm square	Cut 4
b	5cm × 59cm 5cm × 27cm	Cut 4 each
c	5cm square	Cut 1
d	5cm square	Cut 4

Quilt batting }
Lining } 71cm square each

Strip for binding

4 [d]

284

5.5
5 d
b
59
27
5
a
27
Appliqué

RIO   NANA

Outline stitch with
3 strands of floss in navy.

4.5

C

Quilting

71

SAITOH'S
HOUSE
22, MAY
1982.
by NORTH-
WESTHOME

1.5 2 1.5

71

Binding

Fold

Continued from page 31

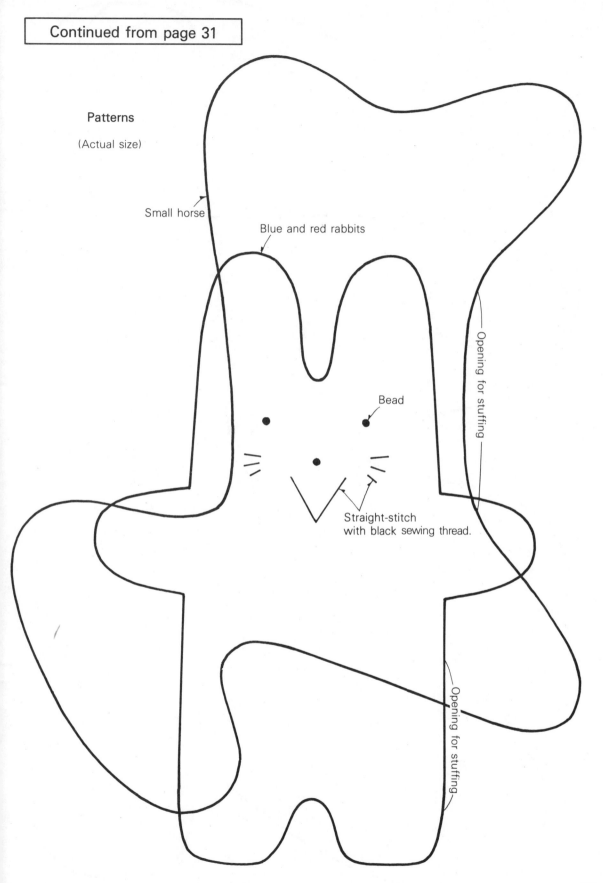

Patterns

(Actual size)

Small horse

Blue and red rabbits

Bead

Opening for stuffing

Straight-stitch
with black sewing thread.

Opening for stuffing

Patterns   (Actual size)

Large horse

Green rabbit

Bead

Draw with red pencil.

Straight-stitch with
black sewing thread.

Outline-stitch with
2 strands of floss in red.

Opening for stuffing

Open
pattern from
fold line.

Opening for stuffing

Open pattern
from fold line.

89

MATERIALS

FABRIC: Cotton prints: 12 pieces of 8.5 cm by 16.5 cm.
Felt: Scraps of red, white, pink and black. Glue. Rouge.
Quilt batting. Polyester fiberfill. Green ribbon, 1.2 cm
by 60 cm. 70 cm wire. Round beads (small): 2 black and
1 red.
FINISHED SIZE: See diagram.

DIRECTIONS:

Make 12 puffs following diagram. Arrange puffs so that
colors harmonize. Insert wire into center of puffs using
awl and twist ends. Twist ends of wire to make hanger.
Make Santa Claus and sew on. Sew on bow.

Making puffs

Cut out 12 pieces of
8.5 cm by 16.5 cm
each.

Turn in seam allowance and
run a gathering stitch.
Pull thread.
0.5 cm

Stuff with
fiberfill loosely.

Pull thread.

(Wrong side) 8.5 cm
16.5 cm
0.4 cm
0.7 cm

4 cm

Fold in half with right
sides together and sew
sides with 0.7 cm seam.
Turn inside out.

Stitch in same way.

Make 11 puffs in same way.

Thread 12 puffs onto wire
so that colors harmonize.
Twist wires to make
hanger.

Santa Claus

Patterns (Actual size)

No seam allowance for felt.

Mustache
White

Head
Cut 2 in pink

3 cm

Tie ribbon into
bow and
sew on.

20 cm

Sew on
Santa Claus

Overcast

Overcast

Cap
Red

Black button

Gown Red

Pants
Red

Sew on center
back of gown.

Glove White

Arm Cut 1 in red

Shoes Black

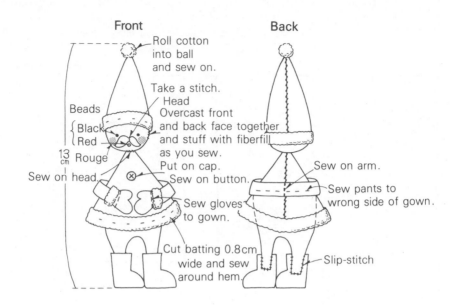

Front

Roll cotton into ball and sew on.

Take a stitch.

Head

Overcast front and back face together and stuff with fiberfill as you sew.

Beads
{ Black
{ Red

Put on cap.

13 cm Rouge

Sew on button.

Sew on head.

Sew gloves to gown.

Cut batting 0.8cm wide and sew around hem.

Back

Sew on arm.

Sew pants to wrong side of gown.

Slip-stitch

 X'mas Pillows, shown on pages 32 & 33.

MATERIALS

FABRIC: Cotton prints: FOR PILLOW ON PAGE 32: (a) white with design, 50 cm by 30 cm; (b) red with design, 30 cm square; (c) dots; (d) green with design, 25 cm by 12 cm each; (e) green, 42 cm by 38 cm. FOR PILLOW ON PAGE 33: (a-d) same prints as above but the following amounts: (a) 45 cm square; (b) 30 cm square; (c) 24 cm square; (d) 35 cm square; (e) red, 42 cm by 38 cm; (f) small amount of dark green. Quilt batting and backing, 38 cm square each. White quilting thread. White embroidery floss, No. 25. 30 cm zipper. 38 cm-square inner pillow stuffed with kapok.

FINISHED SIZE: 36 cm square.

DIRECTIONS:

1. Cut out patches and sew them together by hand.
2. Draw quilting lines. Pin and baste top, batting and backing together and quilt.
3. Embroider.
4. Sew zipper to back pieces.
5. Sew front and back together with right sides facing. Zigzag-stitch along raw edges by machine. Turn inside out.
6. Insert inner pillow.

Embroidery patterns

(Actual size)

Chain-stitch with 3 strands of floss in white.

Merry

X'mas

Front

Add 0.7cm seam allowance unless otherwise indicated.
Cut 37.5cm square each from batting and backing.

Left pillow

Right Pillow

Back
Cut 2
e

36

18

Zipper

Add 2cm seam allowance.

Piecing

Left pillow

Right pillow

Detail of corner

Machine-stitch inward at corners, so that corners don't jut out after being stuffed.

0.7

5

5

1.5

1.5

0.7 Seam allowance

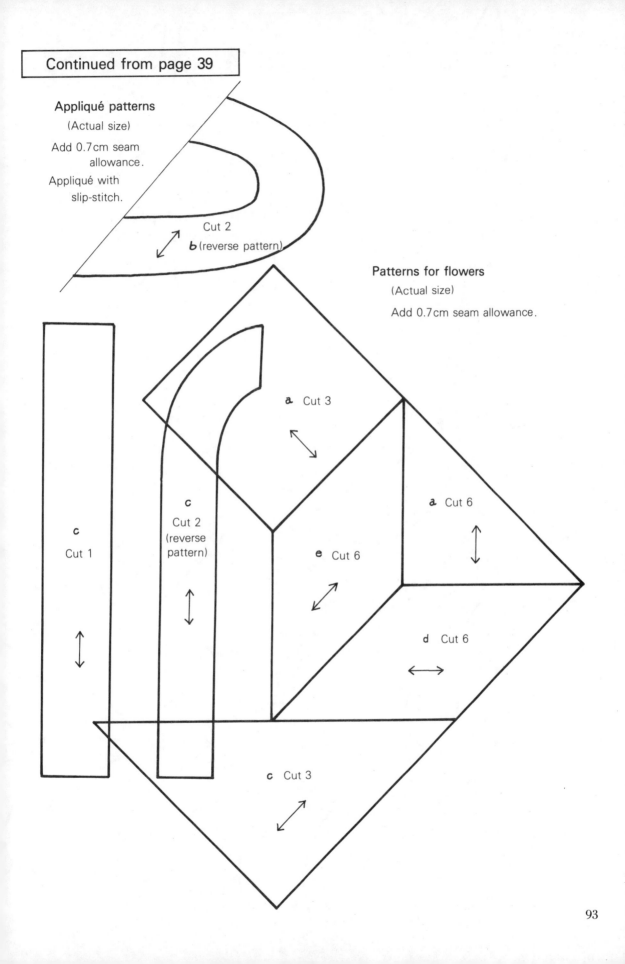

Continued from page 39

Appliqué patterns

(Actual size)

Add 0.7cm seam allowance.

Appliqué with slip-stitch.

Cut 2

b (reverse pattern)

Patterns for flowers

(Actual size)

Add 0.7cm seam allowance.

a Cut 3

a Cut 6

c
Cut 2
(reverse pattern)

c
Cut 1

e Cut 6

d Cut 6

c Cut 3

Quilting patterns
(Actual size)
Stitch with white thread.

Center →

Quilting patterns

(Actual size)

Stitch with navy thread

Center →

Continued from page 47

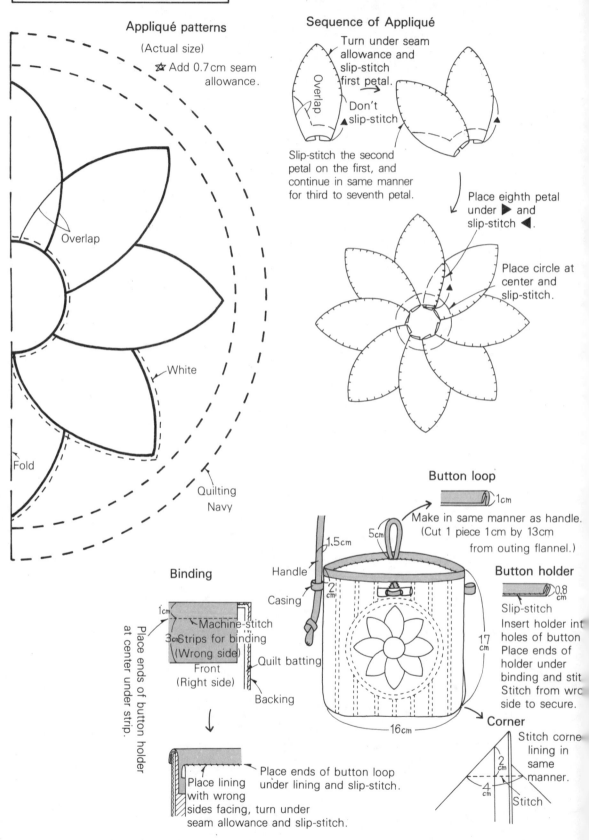

Appliqué patterns

(Actual size)

☆ Add 0.7 cm seam allowance.

Overlap

White

Fold

Quilting Navy

Sequence of Appliqué

Turn under seam allowance and slip-stitch first petal.

Overlap

Don't ▲ slip-stitch

Slip-stitch the second petal on the first, and continue in same manner for third to seventh petal.

Place eighth petal under ▶ and slip-stitch ◀.

Place circle at center and slip-stitch.

Binding

1cm

Machine-stitch
3cm Strips for binding (Wrong side)

Front (Right side)

Quilt batting

Backing

Place ends of button holder at center under strip.

Place lining with wrong sides facing, turn under seam allowance and slip-stitch.

Place ends of button loop under lining and slip-stitch.

Handle

Casing

1.5cm

5cm

2 cm

17 cm

16cm

Button loop

1cm

Make in same manner as handle. (Cut 1 piece 1cm by 13cm from outing flannel.)

Button holder

0.8 cm

Slip-stitch

Insert holder int[o] holes of button Place ends of holder under binding and stit[ch] Stitch from wr[ong] side to secure.

Corner

Stitch corne[r] lining in same manner.

2 cm

4 cm

Stitch

96

Purses, shown on page 44.

MATERIALS

FABRIC: Cotton fabric: (a) 60cm by 45cm (black for Black Purse and red for Red Purse); (b-e) (see photo), 90cm by 10cm each; for backing, 42cm by 47cm; for lining, 62cm by 42cm. Quilt batting, 42cm by 47cm. Quilting thread: black for Black Purse and red for Red Purse. One pair of handles, 29cm long.

FINISHED SIZE: See diagram.

DIRECTIONS:

1. Cut out fabric following diagram. Sew patches together by hand. Make front and back.

2. Sew border to top of front and back individually. Draw quilting lines.
3. Pin and baste top, batting and backing together. Quilt.
4. Sew inside pocket to lining.
5. Pin and baste quilted piece and lining with wrong sides facing. Bind side edges.
6. With wrong sides facing, bind edges of front and back together.
7. Insert top border into handle, turn in seam allowance and slip-stitch.

97

MATERIALS

FABRICS: Cotton fabric: (a) 80 cm by 32 cm (Off-white for Bag at left and Lavender for Bag at right); (b) 90 cm by 65 cm (dark brown for left Bag and purple for right Bag); (c-f) 16 cm square each; for backing, 85 cm by 32 cm; for lining, 72 cm by 50 cm. Quilt batting, 85 cm by 32 cm. Outing flannel, 90 cm by 15 cm. Quilting thread: white and brown for left Bag and white for right Bag. One 5 cm-long bamboo button. Cardboard, same size as bottom.

FINISHED SIZE: See diagram.

DIRECTIONS:

1. Cut out patches for front. Appliqué handles and sew patches together by hand.

2. Sew front, gussets and back together, following diagram. Draw quilting lines.
3. Pin and baste top, batting and backing together. Quilt diagonally. Pin and baste pieces for bottom together and quilt diagonally in two directions.
4. Sew side seams. Sew inside pocket to lining. Sew pieces of lining together in same manner.
5. With wrong sides facing, place quilted piece on lining. Bind edges of body and bottom together.
6. Make handles, button loop and button holder following directions on page 46, 47 and 96. Bind edges of opening, catching ends of handles, loop and holder.
7. Place cardboard on bottom.

(   ) shows seam allowance.
[   ] shows left bag, <   > shows right bag and same color unless otherwise indicated.
Cut out quilt batting, lining and backing, 71.5 cm by 31.5 cm each.

98

Patterns (Actual size) Add 0.7 cm seam allowance.

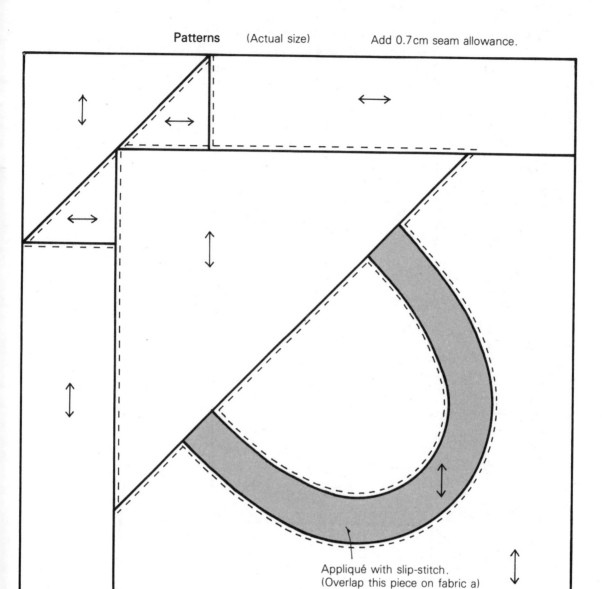

Appliqué with slip-stitch.
(Overlap this piece on fabric a)

Tea Cozy and Matching Mat,
shown on page 49.

MATERIALS

FABRIC: Cotton fabric: FOR TEA COZY: (a) red with floral design, 35 cm square; (b) red, 50 cm by 60 cm; (c) small amount of white with floral design. FOR MAT: Same as Tea Cozy: (a) 35 cm square; (b) 50 cm by 30 cm; (d) small amount. Polyester fiberfill.

FINISHED SIZE: See diagram.

DIRECTIONS FOR TEA COZY:

1. Cut patches for front and one piece of back adding seam allowance. Sew patches together by hand.

2. With wrong sides facing, sew bottom seams of top and lining. Insert fiberfill.
3. Make loop.
4. Bind edges of front and back together catching ends of loop placed on back.

FOR MAT:

1. Work same as Tea Cozy.
2. Place fiberfill thinly between top and lining. Bind edges.

Patterns (Actual size)   Add 0.7 cm seam allowance.

Tea cozy.....Top piece (Patchwork), Lining (Fabirc b).....Cut 2 each.

Mat.....Top piece (Patchwork), Lining (Fabric a).....Cut 1 each.

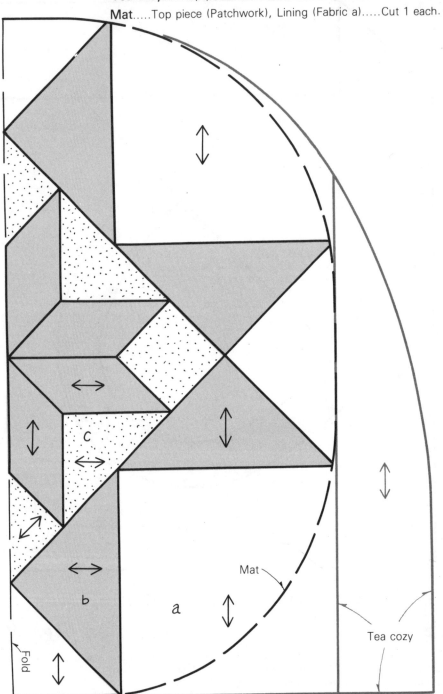

c

b

a

Fold

Mat

Tea cozy

Strips for binding Cut 1 each

3

b

Tea cozy = **54**
Mat = **62**

Loop

3

b

6.5

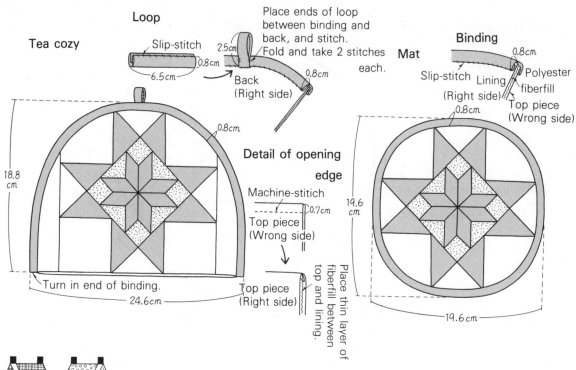

Tea cozy

Loop

Slip-stitch

6.5cm 0.8cm

2.5cm

Place ends of loop between binding and back, and stitch. Fold and take 2 stitches each.

Back (Right side)

0.8cm

0.8cm

Mat

Binding

0.8cm

Slip-stitch Lining (Right side)

Polyester fiberfill

Top piece (Wrong side)

0.8cm

Detail of opening edge

Machine-stitch

0.7cm

Top piece (Wrong side)

Top piece (Right side)

Place thin layer of fiberfill between top and lining.

18.8 cm

0.8cm

Turn in end of binding.

24.6cm

19.6 cm

19.6 cm

Duck Crib Quilt, shown on page 40.

Add 1cm seam allowance to patches.
Fold quilt batting in half to make 120cm by 92.5cm.
Fold excess when binding.

Cut out lining, 91cm by 118cm.

5
13.5
13.5
19
19

5

19 White

White background

Appliqué

Back Front

Buggy

27

Quilt with 3 strands of floss in yellow

Binding

1.5

1.5

4
4

118

91

MATERIALS
FABRICS: Cotton broadcloth: White, 90cm square; white with small flowers, 85cm by 65cm; yellow with small flowers, 50cm by 110cm; for lining, 91cm by 118cm. Cotton fabric for appliques: Light yellow, 75cm by 40cm; orange, 30cm square; small amount of blue. Quilt batting, 120cm by 185cm. Embroidery floss, No. 25: 2 skeins of yellow and small amount of charcoal gray.
FINISHED SIZE: 118cm by 91cm.
DIRECTIONS:
1. Cut patches adding 1cm seam allowance and sew them together by machine.
2. Cut appliques adding 0.7cm seam allowance. Appliqué in place using slip-stitch.

Strips for binding

12

Yellow background

110
93 Cut 2 each

See page 2 for finishing corners.

3. Draw quilting lines on top. Pin and baste top, batting and lining together and quilt.
4. Bind edges to finish.

Duck

Cut 7 for front.

Cut 3 for back.

Satin stitch with 2 strands of floss in charcoal gray.

Appliqué patterns (Actual size)

Add 0.7 cm seam allowance.

Don't sew mouth and eyes on back.

Buggy Cut 2

Blue

Light yellow

Orange

Potholders, shown on page 53.

OCTAGON
MATERIALS
FABRICS: Cotton fabric: Brick red, 30 cm square; unbleached, 25 cm square; green, 10 cm by 20 cm; green and white stripes, 12 cm by 22 cm; backing, 18 cm square.

Outing flannel, 36 cm by 18 cm. Dark brown quilting thread.
FINISHED SIZE: See diagram.
DIRECTIONS: Make in same manner as Potholders on page 54.

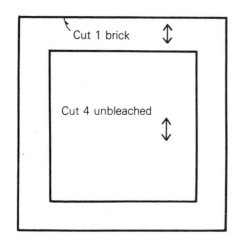

Cut 1 brick

Cut 4 unbleached

Patterns (Actual size)
Add 0.7 cm seam allowance.

Cut 4 stripes

Cut 4 green
(Reverse pattern
of stripes)

Front

Top piece (Patchwork) See patterns.
Outing flannel ⎫ Cut 1 each same
Backing ⎭ size as back.

16

16

0.5

Quilting

Back

Top piece unbleached ⎫ Cut 1 each.
Outing flannel ⎭

4.5

4.5

18 9

2.5
2.5

Quilting

18

Strips for binding

4 ☒ Brick

64

Hanging loop

4 ☒ Brick

8

Hanging loop

1cm

Turn in seam allowances
and machine-stitch.

3cm

Fold strip in half, insert
ends of loop under binding
and
slip-stitch.

Binding with
1cm wide
strips.

Turn in end.

18
cm

9 cm

18 cm

MITTEN
MATERIALS
FABRICS: Cotton fabric: Red with yellow stars, 45 cm by 40 cm; small amount each of unbleached, mustard, and green; for lining, 40 cm by 24 cm. Outing flannel, 60 cm by 24 cm. Red sewing thread.
FINISHED SIZE: See diagram.
DIRECTIONS:
1. Place one piece of outing flannel between top and lining of front and place two pieces of outing flannel for back. Pin and baste. Quilt by machine.
2. Sew patches together following directions on page 105 and machine-stitch patches to front with tapes.
3. With right sides facing, sew front and back together. Overcast raw edges to prevent fraying.
4. Turn inside out. Bind edges of opening, catching ends of loop.

Patterns (Actual size)

Add 1 cm seam allowance unless otherwise indicated.

Top piece.....Red ⎱ Cut 2 each
Lining ⎰ reverse pattern

Outing flannel Cut 3

2.5

2.5

Quilting

( ) shows seam allowance.
No seam allowance unless otherwise indicated.

Tape

(0.6)

| Mustard | |
| Green | } Cut 1 each ↕ |

(0.6)

1.2

19

Bias-cut strips

⊠

Red

4

Hanging loop = 10 ⎱ Cut 1 each
Opeing = 26 ⎰

Patches, Tapes

No seam allowance for opening.

Piecing (by machine)

1. Cut fabric

3.4 | Cut 2 unbleached | ↕
|---|---|

|←——— 31 ———→|

2.6 | Green / Mustard | Cut 1 each ↕

2. Work in alphabetical order

Unbleached | 1.2 cm | (a) Sew pieces together with 0.7 cm seams.
Mustard
Green
| 1.2 cm |

3.1 cm | 3.1 cm

(b) cut vertically to make 3.1 cm-wide pieces (cut 10).

3. Sew pieced strips together with 0.7 cm seams.

7.8 cm | 1.7 cm | 1.7 cm

4.

(c) Trim excess along each side after sewing onto front.

End of pattern

(a) Trim excess to make 5.4 cm-wide strip.

(b) Turn in seam allowance of tape, place on pieced strip and baste.

3.4 cm

17.5 cm

22.5 cm

Green

Mustard

3.4 cm

Machine-stitch

1 cm wide binding with bias-cut strip.

Fold in half, place ends of loop between front and binding and stitch.

4 cm

1 cm

Hanging loop Turn in bias-cut strip and machine-stitch.

Muffler,
shown on pages
60 & 61.

MATERIALS

FABRICS: Wool; (a-b) 34 cm by 40 cm each. Fabric for lining, 32 cm by 146 cm. White quilting thread.

FINISHED SIZE: 30 cm by 144 cm.

DIRECTIONS:

1. Cut out patches and sew them together by machine.
2. With right sides facing, sew pieced top and lining together, leaving opening for turning. Turn inside out and slip-stitch opening closed.
3. Quilt along seams of each patch.

Add 1 cm seam allowance.

Cut out lining, 32 cm by 146 cm.

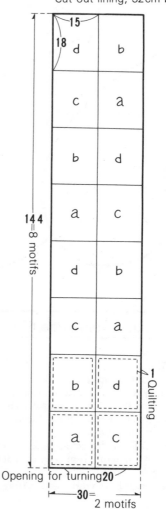

15

18 | d | b

c | a

b | d

144
8 motifs | a | c

d | b

c | a

b | d

1 Quilting

a | c

Opening for turning 20

|←——— 30 ———→|
2 motifs

105

Continued from page 59

Quilting patterns

(Actual size)

Pattern of border
strip corners.

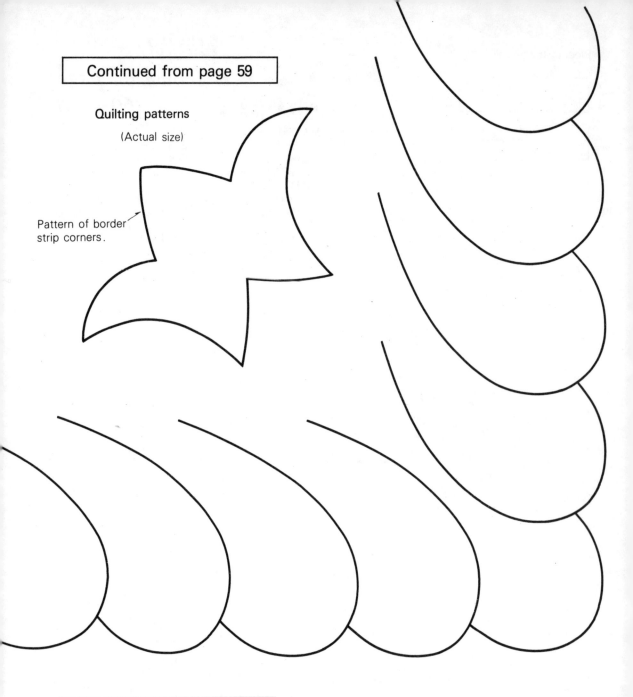

Continued from page 63

Child's Happi Coat
MATERIALS
FABRICS: Cotton fabric: (g) pink, 90 cm square; (h) rose
pink, 50 cm by 40 cm; (a-f) small amount of each. Fabrics
for backing and lining, 90 cm square each. Quilt batting, 90 cm square. Red quilting thread. Embroidery
floss, No. 25: purple and blue.
FINISHED SIZE: Width across back, 42 cm. Length,
44 cm. Sleeve length from center back, 38 cm.
DIRECTIONS:
1. Cut out pieces from fabrics and batting.

2. Cut out appliques. Appliqué leaves on front. Make
   10 pieces of yo-yo flowers and sew in place.
3. Sew center back seams of top and lining individually. Press seams open.
4. Draw quilting lines on top. Pin and baste top, batting and backing together. Quilt.
5. Quilt along leaves. Embroider.
6. Make in same manner as Mother's Happi Coat for
   10—12 on page 63.

Cut out left piece (reverse pattern)

Cut one left and right quilt batting and backing as one continuous piece without seam allowance at center back.
Cut lining same size as top piece.

Strips for binding

Grape

(Yo-yo)

c Cut 8
d Cut 6
e Cut 4
f Cut 2

0.3 seam allowance

5

See page 19 for making instructions.

2.2

Appliqué patterns (Actual size)   Add 0.5cm seam allowance.   **Leave** Cut 2 each.

Quilt along appliqué.   Outline stitch with 2 strands of floss. (Cut out other one by reverse pattern)

Purple   Blue

a   b

Appliqué with slip-stitch.

MATERIALS

FABRICS: Cotton broadcloth: Off-white with wild berries, 90 cm by 50 cm; off-white, 90 cm by 36 cm; brown, 90 cm by 10 cm. Quilt batting, 31 cm by 25 cm. Outing flannel, 90 cm by 12 cm. Brown embroidery floss, No. 25. Elastic tape, 1.4 cm by 40 cm. Cardboard, 31 cm by 25 cm.
FINISHED SIZE: See diagram.

DIRECTIONS:

Cut fabrics and batting. Pin and baste top, batting and backing together. Appliqué on top, catching backing. Sew bias-cut strip to edges. Place cardboard and lining on backing. Bind edges of all pieces in slip-stitch. Make handles and sew in place. Braid tapes and sew on in slip stitch.

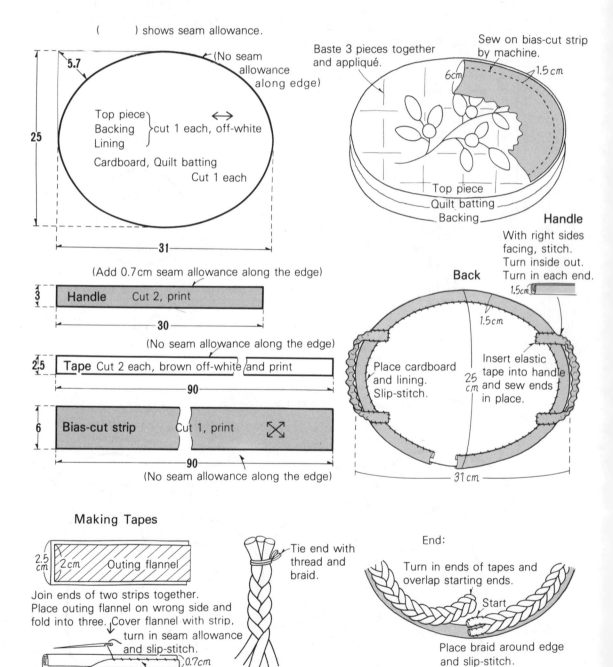

( ) shows seam allowance.

5.7
(No seam allowance along edge)
25
Top piece ⎫
Backing ⎬ cut 1 each, off-white
Lining ⎭
Cardboard, Quilt batting Cut 1 each
31

(Add 0.7 cm seam allowance along the edge)
3
Handle   Cut 2, print
30

(No seam allowance along the edge)
2.5
Tape Cut 2 each, brown off-white and print
90

6
Bias-cut strip   Cut 1, print
90
(No seam allowance along the edge)

Baste 3 pieces together and appliqué.
Sew on bias-cut strip by machine.
6cm
1.5 cm
Top piece
Quilt batting
Backing

Handle
With right sides facing, stitch. Turn inside out. Turn in each end.
1.5 cm

Back
1.5 cm
Place cardboard and lining. Slip-stitch.
Insert elastic tape into handle and sew ends in place.
25 cm
31 cm

Making Tapes

2.5 cm 2cm Outing flannel

Join ends of two strips together. Place outing flannel on wrong side and fold into three. Cover flannel with strip, turn in seam allowance and slip-stitch.
0.7cm
Slip-stitch.

Tie end with thread and braid.

End:
Turn in ends of tapes and overlap starting ends.
Start
Place braid around edge and slip-stitch.

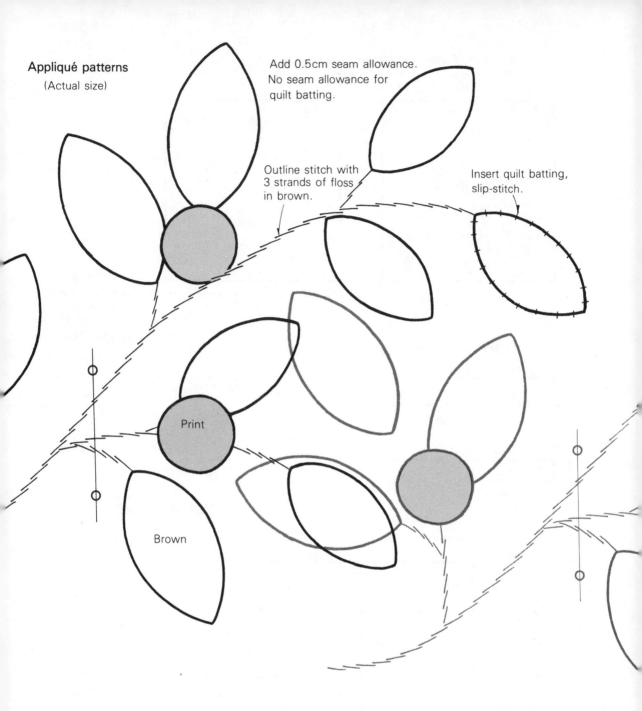

Appliqué patterns
(Actual size)

Add 0.5cm seam allowance.
No seam allowance for
quilt batting.

Outline stitch with
3 strands of floss
in brown.

Insert quilt batting,
slip-stitch.

Print

Brown

 Cosmetic Cases, shown on pages 68 & 69.

MATERIALS (FOR ONE)
FABRIC: Cotton fabric: Off-white, 45 cm by 25 cm; small
amount each of 5 different prints and solids (see photo);
for lining, 19 cm by 37.5 cm. Quilt batting, 19.5 cm by
37.5 cm. White quilting thread. 18 cm zipper for B. One
button, 1.5 cm in diameter for C.
FINISHED SIZE: See diagram.

DIRECTIONS:
1. Cut fabric. Appliqué stem. Sew patches together by
   hand.
2. Sew bottom seams of front and back. Draw quilting
   lines. Pin and baste top and batting. Quilt.
3. Sew side seams with right sides together. Sew side
   seams of lining. Sew corners of bottom for B. Finish
   following diagrams on next page.

Add 0.7cm seam allowance unless otherwise indicated.
Cut out 1 piece of quilt batting, 19.5cm by 37.4cm.
Cut out 1 piece of lining, 19cm by 37.4cm.

Front

4.5 9 4.5

Off-white

0.4 Quilting

18

18

2.5 2.5

Quilting

Back

Off-white

18

Opening

With right sides together, stitch.

Strip for binding (Wrong side)

Front (Right side)

Place zipper on right side of strip and sew on with back stitch.

0.7cm 0.7cm

Slip-stitch
Lining
(Right side)

(Wrong side)

B

Strips for binding

(No seam allowance along edge)

2.8 Off-white

38

Button loop of C

(No seam allowance along edge)

2 Off-white

10

Zipper

16 cm

14cm

See page 71 for corner.

Patterns (Actual size)

Add 0.7cm seam allowance.

Appliqué with slip-stitch

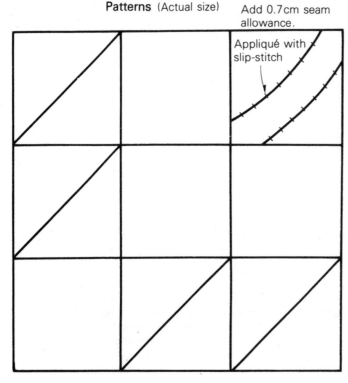

C: See page 71 for opening and button loop.

Loop

Button

18 cm

18 cm

Pen Case, shown on pages 68 & 69.

MATERIALS
FABRIC: Blue-gray, 16 cm by 40 cm; print, 35 cm square; for lining, 9 cm by 40 cm. Quilt batting, 9 cm by 40 cm. White quilting thread. One snap fastener.
FINISHED SIZE: See diagram.
DIRECTIONS:
1. Cut fabric. Sew patches together by hand.
2. Draw quilting lines on top. Pin and baste top, batting and lining together. Quilt.
3. Bind straight edges. Fold in half with wrong sides together. Bind edges all around except bottom.
4. Sew on snap fastener.

Add 0.7 cm seam allowance.
Cut quilt batting and lining same size as top piece.

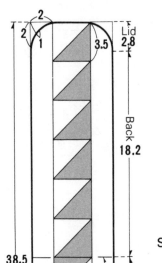

Strip for binding   No seam allowance.

Glasses Case, shown on page 69.

MATERIALS
FABRIC: Cotton fabric: Dotted print, 40 cm by 20 cm; beige, 40 cm square; small amount each of 8 different prints and solids for patches (see photo). Quilt batting, 23 cm by 20 cm. White quilting thread.
FINISHED SIZE: 11.5 cm by 19.5 cm.

DIRECTIONS:
1. Cut fabric. Sew patches together by hand.
2. Draw quilting lines on front and back. Pin and baste front, batting and lining together. Baste back pieces in same manner. Quilt.
3. Bind top edges of front and back individually. With wrong sides facing, bind edges of front and back together.

111

Front (Actual size)

Add 0.7cm seam allowance.

Cut 1 piece of back same size as front in dotted print.
Cut 2 pieces each of quilt batting and lining (beige) same size as front.

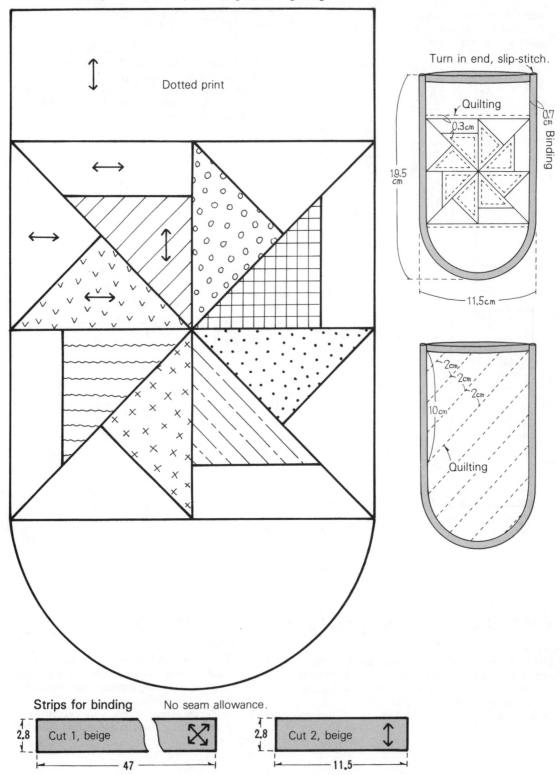

Strips for binding   No seam allowance.

2.8   Cut 1, beige

47

2.8   Cut 2, beige

11.5

MATERIALS

FABRICS: Blue quilted fabric, 23 cm square. Cotton fabric: For appliques, small amount each of 9 different prints and solids; for lining, 23 cm square. White cotton lace edging (gathered), 2.5 cm by 20 cm.

FINISHED SIZE: 7 cm by 21 cm.

DIRECTIONS:

1. Cut fabric. Sew patches together. Appliqué in place.
2. Sew front and back together with right sides facing. Turn inside out. Sew lining in same manner.
3. Insert lining into quilted case with wrong sides together. Place lace edging between top and lining and slip-stitch.

Patterns

(Actual size)

Add 1 cm seam allowance.
Add 0.7 cm seam allowance for appliqué fabric.

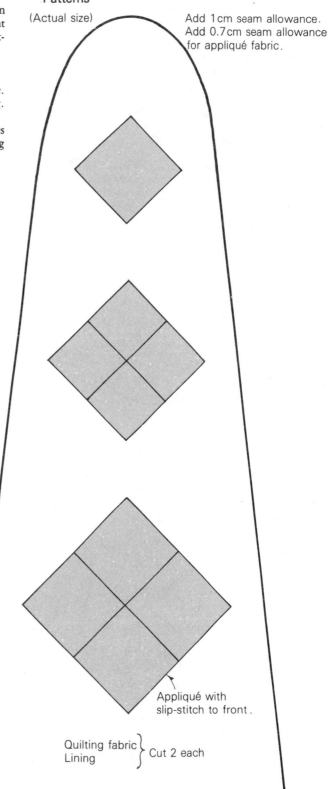

Opening

Top piece (Right side)

Lining (Wrong side)

(b) Slip-stitch.

(c) Slip-stitch

2 cm

(a) Join ends of lace edging. Place between top and lining.

Appliqué with slip-stitch to front.

Quilting fabric
Lining } Cut 2 each

ANGEL
MATERIALS

FABRIC: Cotton fabric: Small amount each of red with white dots and white with red flowers. White felt, 15 cm square. White mohair yarn (extra fine). Red ribbon, 1 cm by 35 cm. Silver spangles: 14 round and 1 star-shaped (large). Round beads: 2 black (medium) and 1 red (small). 15 transparent beads. White cotton lace edging, 1 cm by 25 cm. Polyester fiberfill. Iron-on interfacing. Rouge. Green felt-tipped pen. Glue.

FINISHED SIZE: 12 cm tall.

DIRECTIONS:

1. Cut fabric and felt. Overcast front and back of body together leaving opening for stuffing. Stuff with fiberfill. Slip-stitch opening closed. Make head in same manner.

2. Attach hair to head. Make features.
3. Sew dress.
4. Put dress on body. Sew head to body.
5. Sew 2 pieces of wing together and turn inside out. Stuff with fiberfill and slip-stitch opening closed. Make another wing in same manner.
6. Sew wings to body catching ends of ribbon.
7. Sew bow onto head. Color feet with felt-tip pen for shoes.

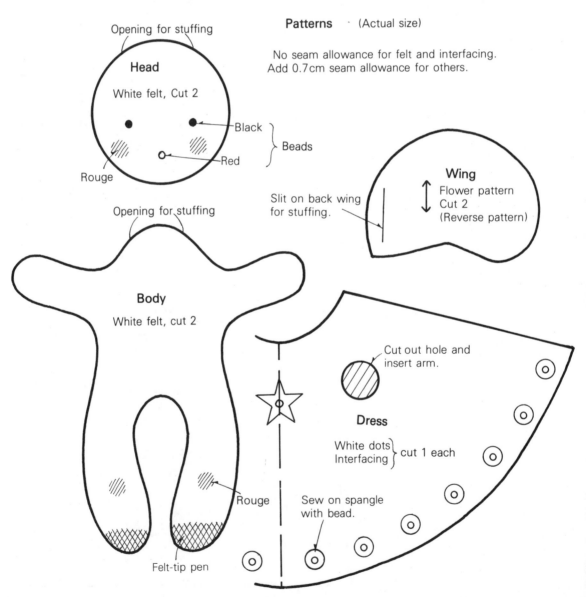

Patterns · (Actual size)

No seam allowance for felt and interfacing.
Add 0.7 cm seam allowance for others.

Opening for stuffing

Head

White felt, Cut 2

Black
Red
Beads

Rouge

Wing
Flower pattern
Cut 2
(Reverse pattern)

Slit on back wing
for stuffing.

Opening for stuffing

Body

White felt, cut 2

Rouge

Felt-tip pen

Cut out hole and
insert arm.

Dress

White dots
Interfacing } cut 1 each

Sew on spangle
with bead.

Hair

Cut 40 strands of 8cm-long yarn.
Sew center of yarn to head.

Trim and glue hair to head.

Tie ribbon — 4cm — 3cm — 4cm —

Fold ribbon into bow and sew onto head.

Fold 24cm ribbon in half and place ends between dress and wings.

Sew on head.

Slip-stitch

12 cm

Slip-stitch

Sew on wings 3.5cm

Slip-stitch

Dress

Make in alphabetical order from (a) to (f).

(b) Turn back seam allowance and glue. 0.6cm

(a) Press iron-on interfacing on wrong side.

(c) Sew lace edging.

(f) Cut out holes.

(d) Sew on spangles with beads.

(e) Overcast

BALL

MATERIALS

FABRIC: Small amount each of 4 different prints. Red ribbon, 1cm by 40cm. Polyester fiberfill.

FINISHED SIZE: 8cm in diameter.

DIRECTIONS:

1. Cut fabric. Sew 3 patches together by hand. Then sew 4 groups of 3 patches together to form ball leaving opening for stuffing.
2. Stuff with fiberfill and slip-stitch opening closed. Sew on bow.

Patterns (Actual size)

Add 0.7cm seam allowance.

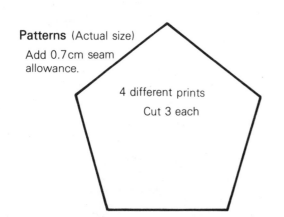

4 different prints
Cut 3 each

Make 4 groups of 3 patches. Sew them together to form ball being careful not to place same design side by side and leaving opening for stuffing.

Fold ribbon in half and sew on. Sew bow onto ribbon.

6.5cm

5.5cm

8cm

BIRD

MATERIALS

FABRIC: Small amount each of 2 different prints (see photo). Yellow felt. Red ribbon, 1 cm by 17 cm. 2 black round spangles (small). 2 white round beads (small). Polyester fiberfill.

FINISHED SIZE: See diagram.

DIRECTIONS:

1. Cut fabric.
2. Sew body and tail together. Sew front and back together with right sides facing and with beak and ends of ribbon in between, leaving opening for stuffing. Turn inside out. Stuff with fiberfill and slip-stitch opening closed.
3. Sew 2 pieces of wing together with right sides facing. Turn inside out. Stuff with fiberfill and slip-stitch slit closed.
4. Sew on wings and spangles with beads.

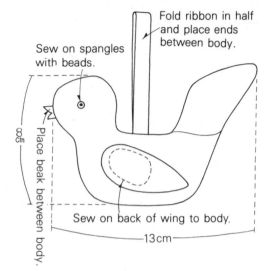

Sew on spangles with beads.

Fold ribbon in half and place ends between body.

Place beak between body.

8 cm

13 cm

Sew on back of wing to body.

Patterns (Actual size)

Add 0.7 cm seam allowance unless otherwise indicated.

Cut 2 pieces of body in reverse pattern.

Tail
Green

Overlapping

Beak
Yellow, cut 1
No seam allowance.

Body   Red

Wing
Green
Cut 2 pieces each in reverse pattern.

Opening for stuffing
Make a slit on back.

Opening for stuffing

HOUSE

MATERIALS

FABRIC: Small amount each of 3 different prints (see photo). Green ribbon, 1 cm by 15 cm. Black embroidery floss, No. 25. Polyester fiberfill.

FINISHED SIZE: 11.5 cm by 8.5 cm.

DIRECTIONS:

1. Cut fabric. Sew patches together by hand.
2. With right sides facing, sew front and back together catching ends of ribbon and leaving opening for stuffing. Turn inside out. Stuff with fiberfill and slip-stitch opening closed.

Fold ribbin in half and place ends between roof.

8.5 cm

Chain stitch with 2 strands of floss in black.

11.5 cm

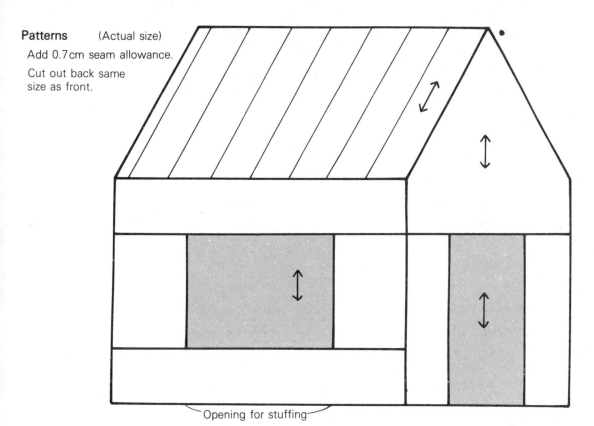

Patterns (Actual size)

Add 0.7cm seam allowance.

Cut out back same size as front.

Opening for stuffing

Electric Cooker Cover,
shown on page 53.

MATERIALS

FABRICS: Mustard quilted fabric, 90cm by 29cm. Cotton fabric: 30cm square each of (a) white and dark brown stripes, (b) dark brown with flowers, (c) moss green with white dots and mustard; 25cm each of red with yellow stars and unbleached; for backing, 30cm square. Quilt batting, 30cm square. Dark brown binding tape, 92cm long. White quilting thread.

FINISHED SIZE: See diagram.

DIRECTIONS:

1. Cut out patches for top adding seam allowance. Sew them together by hand. Press seams following diagram on next page.
2. Pin and baste top, batting and backing together. Quilt.
3. Cut out patches for side adding seam allowance. Sew them together by hand.
4. Zigzag-stitch raw edges of side by machine. Sew side seams. Turn in seam allowance of bottom and sew together with right sides facing and binding tape in between. Zigzag-stitch raw edges.

Top

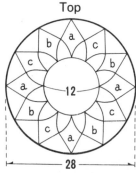

Cut out backing and quilt batting, 30cm in diameter.

Side

117

Piecing for Top

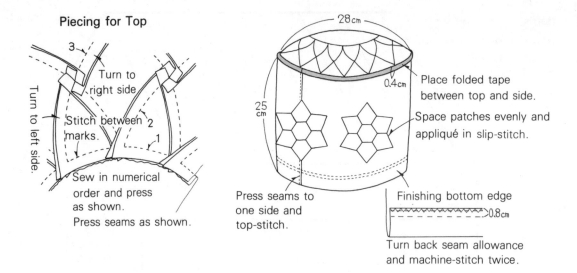

3

Turn to right side.

Turn to left side.

Stitch between marks.

2

1

Sew in numerical order and press as shown.
Press seams as shown.

28cm

0.4cm

25 cm

Place folded tape between top and side.

Space patches evenly and appliqué in slip-stitch.

Press seams to one side and top-stitch.

Finishing bottom edge

0.8cm

Turn back seam allowance and machine-stitch twice.

Patterns (Actual size)

Add 0.7cm seam allowance.

a..... Stripes
b.... Dark brown
c..... White dots

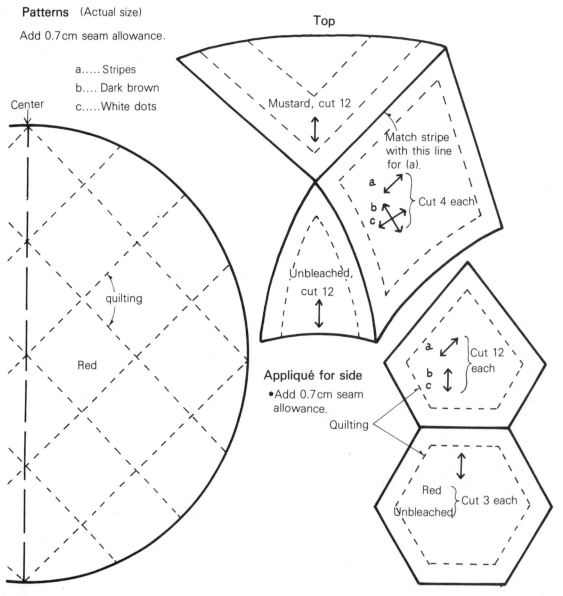

Center

quilting

Red

Top

Mustard, cut 12

Match stripe with this line for (a).

a
b
c

Cut 4 each

Unbleached, cut 12

a
b
c

Cut 12 each

Appliqué for side

• Add 0.7cm seam allowance.

Quilting

Red
Unbleached

Cut 3 each

Toaster Oven Cover, shown on page 52.

MATERIALS

FABRICS: Mustard quilted fabric, 70cm by 65cm. Cotton fabric: Red with yellow stars, 55cm by 25cm; dark brown with white dots and unbleached, 55cm by 20cm each.

FINISHED SIZE: See diagram.

DIRECTIONS:

1. Sew patches together. Sew pieced patches onto front and back with tapes.

2. Appliqué 3 patches on top. Zigzag-stitch raw edges by machine.

3. Bind top edge of pocket. Tie ribbon into bow and sew onto pocket.

4. Sew bottom of pocket onto gusset. Zigzag-stitch raw edges.

5. Sew gussets, front and back together with right sides facing. Turn back seam allowance of bottom and machine-stitch.

( ) shows seam allowance.

Back

Top — Quilted fabric Cut 1

Front — Tape

Tape
Red
Dark brown — Cut 2 each

Pocket
Quilted fabric Cut 1
(No seam allowance)

Gusset
Quilted fabric Cut 2

Strip for binding
Red Cut 1

Ribbon
Red cut 1
(Add 0.5cm seam allowance along edges)

Appliqué pieces
Dark brown, Red, Unbleached
Cut 1 each
(Add 0.7cm seam allowance along edges)

Appliqué with slip-stitch.

Red · Dark brown · Unbleached

Piecing (by machine)

(1) Cut fabric

Unbleached, Red, Dark brown Cut 2 each — 54

(2) Pieces in alphabetical order.

Unbleached / Red / Dark brown

(a) Sew unbleached, red and dark brown fabrics together with 0.7cm seams.

(b) Cut into 5.4cm-wide strips (Cut 10).

(3) Sew pieced strips together with 0.7cm seams.

(4) Trim excess to make one piece. Place tape along dash line. 47cm by 7.6cm. Trim excess.

(5) Repeat steps 2 to 4 to make another strip.

Top edge of pocket
1cm wide binding with strips.
Tie ribbon into bow and sew on to pocket.
Turn in seam allowances and machine stitch.
Turn back seam allowance of pocket's bottom and machine stitch.

Sew pieced patches with tapes.

Dark brown · Red

Finishing bottom edge
Turn back seam allowance of bottom and machine-stitch.

119

Sewing Box, shown on page 72.

MATERIALS

FABRIC: Cotton broadcloth: (a-k). Small amount each of 11 different prints and solids (see photo). Empty box, 23.5 cm by 15.5 cm by 6.7 cm. Quilt batting, 23.5 cm by 15.5 cm. Heavy-duty white cotton sewing thread for quilting. white cotton lace edging (gathered), 2.5 cm by 80 cm. Gray thick paper. Glue.

DIRECTIONS:

1. Cut out patches and background fabric for lid. Sew patches together by hand.
2. Appliqué pieced patches to foundation blocks with running stitch. Sew blocks together by hand. Pin and baste top and batting together. Quilt along seams of center square. Bind edges.

Lid   (Actual size)

No seam allowance along edges. Cut out adding 0.5 cm seam allowance unless edges.
Cut out background fabric (a~c) continuing shaded part.
Quilt batting 23.5 × 15.5 cm

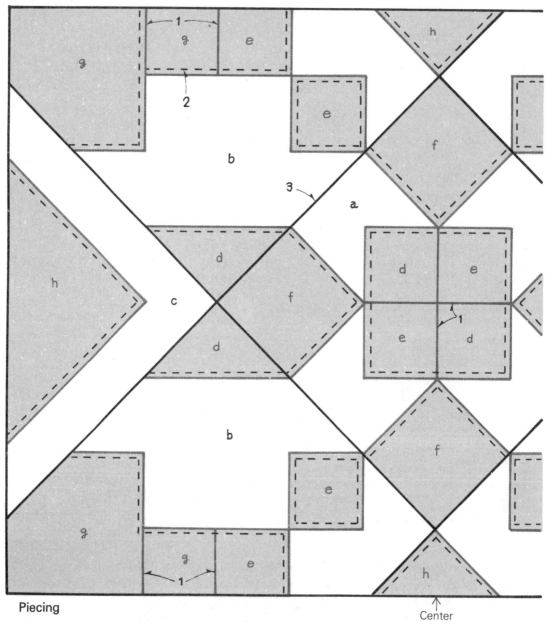

Piecing

1. Sew patches together by hand.

2. Appliqué pieced patches (d~h) to foundation blocks (a~c) with running stitch.

3. Sew blocks together by hand.

120

3. Glue lace edging around lid. Glue quilted top onto lid.
4. Cut out pieces for sides. Sew them together alternating 2 different prints. Sew side seams.

5. Glue pieced sides onto box.

Strips for edge

2.8

i

↕

15.5
25.5 Cut 2 each

Bind raw edges and stitch with white sewing thread.

Detail of edge

Turn in 1cm seam allowance. Strips for edge.

0.7cm

Glue lid

2cm

Glue lace

0.7cm
0.5cm

Adjust inside box.

Sew ends

Lace edging 2cm 0.7cm

Quilt on quilt batting along seams of center square.

0.7cm

Side

Sew with 0.5cm seams and press seams open 1.5 Seam allowance

j   k

Depth = 6

Divide into 7 equal parts — Divide into 5 equal parts
1.5 Seam allowance
Long side = 23.5 — Short side = 15.5

Fold seam allowance and glue.

Bottom
Glue 2 pieces of paper

Glue paper inside

6cm

23.5cm   15.5cm

Pincushion, shown on page 72.

MATERIALS
FABRICS: Off-white with pink flowers, pink with white small flowers, 45cm by 15cm each. Pink cotton broadcloth, 20cm by 17cm. Cotton jersey: Tomato red, 16cm by 8cm; green, 16cm by 10cm. Pink cotton tape, 2cm by 280cm. Peacock green felt. Cotton for stuffing.
FINISHED SIZE: See diagram.
DIRECTIONS:
1. Cut out strips from prints and sew strips and tapes together.
2. Weave tapes to make bottom of basket. Trim excess.

3. Bend tapes and continue to weave side.
4. Sew tape to top edges. Sew on handles.
5. Sew side seams of lining. Insert lining into basket. Turn in seam allowance and slip-stitch lining to basket.
6. Sew 2 pieces of tomato together with right sides facing leaving opening for stuffing. Turn inside out. Stuff with cotton and slip-stitch opening closed. Make avocado in same manner.
7. Sew stem and calyx to tomato.

Tapes

Box 3.4

Pink / Off-white [Box]

Cut 5 each [Handle]

Pink / Off-white [Top edge]

Cut 1 each

Box 21　Handle 16　Top 32

How to make

Cotton tape — Prints — 2cm

Edge machine

Turn back 0.7cm seam allowance and press.

※Sew 2 pieces of tape together for handle.

Turn in end.

Baste.

0.5cm

Turn in end.

Sew on handle and slip-stitch lining.

4.5cm

Tape

Slip-stitch

4.5 cm

6cm　9cm

Basket

Weave in numerical order to make corner. Baste.

17

Bottom

Trim excess after weaving bottom.

14

Off-white

Pink

Lining

1 Seam allowance

4.5

6

Lining
Pink

4.5

Sew together.

4.5　9　4.5

Pincushion (Actual size)

No seam allowance for felt.

Add 0.5cm seam allowance otherwise.

Opening for stuffing

Tomato

Tomato red

Cut 2

Slash and insert stem.

Calyx

Felt

Slip-stitch end of stem.

Seam line

Stem

Avocado

Green

Cut 2

Opening for stuffing

MATERIALS

FABRIC: Sheeting: Peppermint green, 90 cm by 45 cm; mustard, 35 cm by 30 cm; cream and light orange, 23 cm by 18 cm each; pink 17 cm square. Quilt batting, 72 cm by 24 cm.

FINISHED SIZE: 72 cm by 23.5 cm. (Mat)

DIRECTIONS:

1. Sew 9 groups of 5 patches together by machine. Then join groups together.
2. Pin and baste top, batting and lining together. Quilt. Quilt Mat in same manner as Cover.
3. Appliqué telephone cord onto Cover. Bind edges to finish.

Pieces

Add 0.5 cm seam allowance.

a = cut 9 in pink
b = cut 11 in cream
c = cut 11 in light orange
d = cut 7 in mustard
e = cut 2 in peppermint green

b cut 1
c cut 2
d cut 2
e cut 3

Bias-cut strips Peppermint green

No seam allowance.

Cover 102
Mat 82
Appliqué 21

Cover

Top piece.....
Patch pieces
Quilt batting
Lining.....
Peppermint green

Cut 1 each
(Cut out same size as top piece)

Mat

Top piece.....Mustard
Quilt batting
Lining.....Peppermint green

Cut 1 each

Quilting

Binding

Quilt with machine.

Quilt with machine.

Round corner.

0.6 cm
Curve strip and press.
Appliqué in place.

Binding

Bind edges of Mat and Cover with 3.6 cm-wide strip.

Turn in end.

Cover
(Right side)

Bind edges with 1.8 cm-wide strip.

Mat
(Right side)

BASICS IN PATCHWORK

FABRIC: Many small pieces of fabric are sewn together to make patchwork; therefore, fabrics that are too thick, too thin, or that fray easily are not suitable. Medium weight cotton fabrics of plain weave are the most easily handled. New fabrics should be washed to pre-shrink them and remove starch. Press before use.

THREAD: To piece by hand, use cotton or mercerized thread, no. 30-50. If it is not available in colors that match the fabrics, silk thread or embroidery floss may be used. For machine sewing, use a thread that matches the fabric and the machine's gauge.

Cotton thread

Silk sewing thread

Embroidery thread

CUTTING: 1. Make actual-size patterns with cardboard or plastic sheet.

2. Place cardboard patterns on wrong side of fabric and trace around each pattern accurately, leaving a space twice as wide as seam allowance between patterns (about 1 cm—2 cm).
(Cutting pieces accurately is a must for a neat finish.)

Cardboard or plastic sheet

Fabric (Wrong side)

1~2 cm

PIECING: Method A (To piece by using cardboard templates)

This is the most traditional method to sew pieces together. Time and care must be required, but you may have a neater finish.

Make several templates with cardboard (or used postcards). Place template on wrong side of each patch piece and pin.

Turn seam allowances over template and baste, stitching through fabric only.

With right sides facing, overcast edges with tiny stitches.

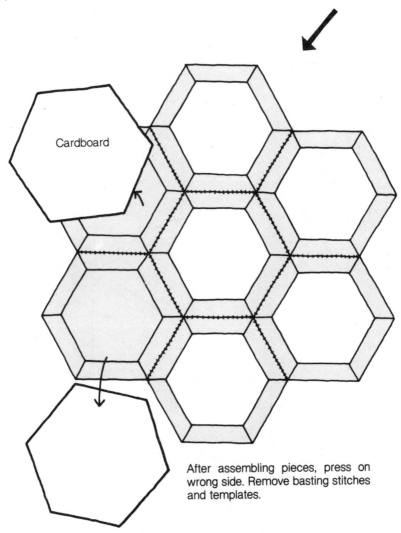

After assembling pieces, press on wrong side. Remove basting stitches and templates.

Method B (To piece by hand)

This is the easiest method for piecing straight seams.
Turn seams to one side.

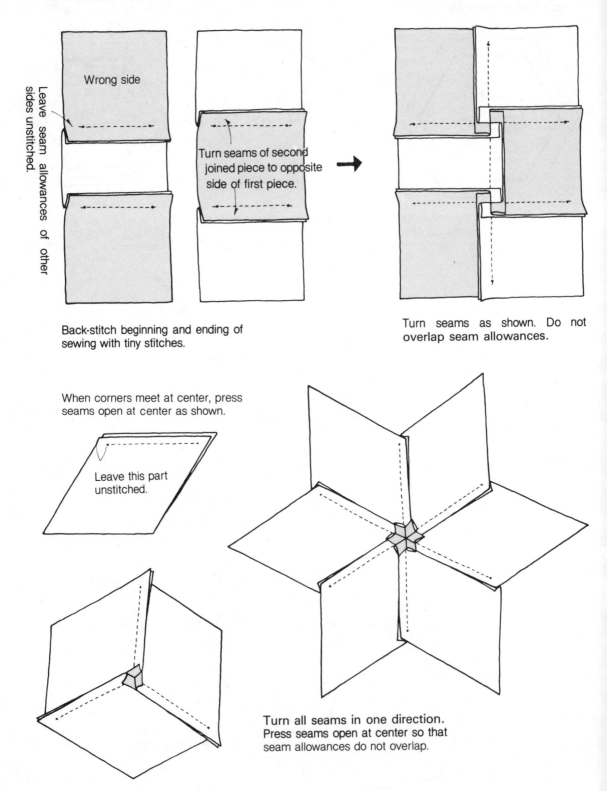

Leave seam allowances of other sides unstitched.

Wrong side

Turn seams of second joined piece to opposite side of first piece.

Back-stitch beginning and ending of sewing with tiny stitches.

Turn seams as shown. Do not overlap seam allowances.

When corners meet at center, press seams open at center as shown.

Leave this part unstitched.

Turn all seams in one direction. Press seams open at center so that seam allowances do not overlap.

Method C (To piece by machine)

Piecing by machine saves time, when you are making a big project. Seams are usually pressed open, but sometimes turned to one side.

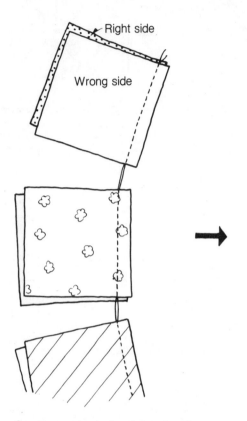

Sew one pair of pieces together by machine and continue to sew pairs of pieces without cutting thread.

Cut thread between pairs and then sew pairs of pieces together.

QUILTING

Quilting is stitching two layers of top piece and lining together with padding between. Cotton and polyester quilt batting or flannel is used for padding. When you quilt by hand using running stitch, push the needle down through all the thicknesses, then push it up again at every stitch for a neater finish.

LINING FABRIC

Soft-finish cotton fabric of loose weave such as sheeting is more easily quilted than closely-woven cotton broadcloth.

Movement of Needle

Push needle down vertically.

Place fabric on quilting pattern and trace, or trace the pattern using tracing paper and cellophane.

Fabric design
Tracing paper
Cellophane
Fabric

Top piece (Right side)
Interlining
Lining

Transfer quilting patterns to right side of top pieces, except pieces to be quilted along seams.
Draw straight lines directly on right side of top pieces with help of ruler.

Place quilt top, batting and lining together and baste three layers. Quilt along quilting lines.

QUILTING METHODS:

Quilt on seams (stitch in the ditch).   Quilt along seams.   Quilt diagonally in two directions.

Quilt along quilting design.

APPLIQUE

Slip-stitch

Seam allowance

Slip-stitch vertically, showing very little stitches.
(Turn in seam allowance at curves with help of needle as you sew.)